HEADTEACHERS AND GOVERNING BODIES

a practical guide to making the partnership work

Martin Pounce

Second edition

Adamson Publishing

© Martin Pounce 2007, 2010

First published in 2007. This edition 2010. Reprinted with updates 2013

Published by Adamson Publishing Ltd
8 The Moorings, Norwich NR3 3AX
tel: 01603 623336 fax: 01603 624767
e-mail: info@adamsonbooks.com
www.adamsonbooks.com

ISBN 9780-948543-92-0

British Library Cataloguing in Publication Data:
A catalogue record for this book is available from the British Library

Cover design by Geoff Shirley

All rights reserved. Individual pages of this book may be photocopied for its own use by a governing body that has purchased the book. With this exception, no part of this publication may be reproduced, stored in a retrieval system, or be transmitted, in any form or by any means, electronic, mechanical, photocopying, recording or otherwise, without the prior permission of the publishers. Such permission, if granted, is subject to a fee depending on the nature of the use.

Printed and bound by Marston Book Services Ltd, Didcot

CONTENTS

Introduction		5
1	Clarifying the Governing Body's Roles	10
2	Principles of Partnership	20
3	Leadership, Governance and Fallibility	24
4	Reporting/Accounting to the Governing Body	28
5	School Self-Evaluation	37
6	Work-Life Balance and Well-Being	40
7	Working with New Relationships	46
8	Deserve What You Get	50
9	Troubleshooting	52
Index and Bibliography		56

The author

Martin Pounce has spent 37 years working in education: as a teacher, teacher-centre leader and, since the mid 1990s, as an education officer in two local authorities. He has been closely involved in governor training and development since 1992 when he joined AGIT (Action for Governors' Information and Training) as Development Officer. Martin has been a governor in two secondary schools in Dudley and Coventry, in a Southwark primary school in the late 1990s and then at an infants school in Buckinghamshire. He is currently chair of governors at a special school and an additional governor in a primary school.

Martin shares his time between work for Oxfordshire Governor Services and consultancy to support colleagues working with governors in other authorities. He writes for a number of publications. He can be contacted via email, martin.pounce@btinternet.com.

Acknowledgements

I acknowledge a huge debt to my wife, Susan, for her encouragement and support; and to all the coordinators and trainers, headteachers and governors with whom I have worked who have sparked ideas and provided examples. My colleagues in Oxfordshire Governor Services, Claudia Wade and Marya Griffiths, have been particularly influential in this respect.

I am very grateful to my editor, Stephen Adamson, for his valiant efforts to keep me focused. The improvements are his; any errors and infelicities that remain are my own.

Martin Pounce
January 2010

INTRODUCTION

There was a time not so long ago (before 1988) when most of the key decisions that affected the development of schools were made by local government officials. Headteachers had little power, and governing bodies even less. When schools were given more autonomy with local management of schools (LMS) under the 1988 Education Reform Act the increased power was not vested in either governing bodies or headteachers but in both working together. And this mirrored arrangements in every area of public life where lay people – whether MPs, councillors, police authorities, health trusts – make and monitor policy in partnership with the professionals.

In the early days of LMS governors and trainers had to assert the legitimacy of governing bodies with headteachers and their staff, many of whom feared interference by governors in professional matters. While professionals on the whole now accept that governing bodies are here to stay, it is not uncommon to hear politicians who should know better stating that the greater autonomy that is being proposed for schools means solely more power for headteachers – "Headteachers will have power over their own admissions, own their own assets and employ their own staff." Even those who know that this is a shorthand for saying "governing bodies with their headteacher will have power" may not be entirely clear about the distinctive roles of governing bodies and what an effective partnership of governing body and headteacher means in practice.

As a governor in six different schools since 1982, and as an officer and sometimes the clerk to governing bodies in Hertfordshire and Oxfordshire since 1995, I have observed and participated in governing body work in more than 100 schools of all shapes and sizes – from a school with 36 pupils to one with over 2000, and special schools too. I have seen governing bodies and headteachers develop and grow together in the confidence with which they address important issues. Mostly, I believe, partnership is developing well, but I have seen some instances of real difficulty. And even where everything does seem to be going well, there are opportunities for improvement. Indeed, there's an urgent need for that improvement if headteachers and governing bodies are to address with confidence some of the key new challenges for the future that will be described in the annex to chapter 1.

DO GOVERNING BODIES PERFORM A USEFUL FUNCTION? ARE THEY WORTH THEIR HEADTEACHER'S TIME?

Most of the 300,000 or so governors in England and Wales certainly think so! They volunteered their time and commitment because they believe they can make a real difference to schools and their pupils. And Ofsted has acknowledged the importance of governance by examining it and commenting on it in the 2012 inspection framework. Within the leadership and management section there is a new judgement on the effectiveness of the governing body in challenging and supporting the school so that weaknesses are tackled decisively and statutory responsibilities met.

However, there are still some headteachers who regard working with governing bodies as a necessary distraction from the real job of leading schools. There are some governors who agree with that notion and fall over themselves to get out of the way. Yet, far from distracting headteachers from the real task of raising standards, governing bodies operating in genuine partnership with them are an integral part of the strategy for achieving those things ... and much else besides.

So, let's all acknowledge our interdependence and seek to do whatever we can to help each other do the best possible job for the sake of our pupils and communities.

National agreement between heads and governors

A two-page statement agreed between the National Governors' Association and the two headteacher associations, *What governing bodies should expect from school leaders and what school leaders should expect from governing bodies,* published in 2008 summarises what each party needs to do to ensure effective working with the other. See www.nga.org.uk.

PARTNERS IN LEADERSHIP AND MANAGEMENT

Some governors find it difficult to judge the right level at which to operate without treading into the headteacher's management territory. Such misunderstanding breeds mistrust which saps the energy of all concerned.

It is with this in mind that I offer this book on the subject of headteachers and governors. The overarching theme of this book is *mutuality and reciprocity*. It is aimed at both headteachers and all other governors and aims to set out:

- how governing bodies can govern so that headteachers can lead

and

- how headteachers can lead so that governing bodies can govern.

Of course, it will be said that governing bodies also lead. There is no suggestion here that governing bodies should abdicate their responsibility for leadership, but it is right to acknowledge that headteachers are full-time leaders (and managers) and, as such, their leadership is distinct from that of governing bodies. Governing body leadership (to which the headteacher, as a governor, contributes) should be about establishing a framework within which the head can exercise confident leadership day by day and month by month, monitoring actions and evaluating the outcomes. But this depends on the information and cooperation offered by the headteacher. So much depends on heads; if they want their governing body to give them space to lead, they must be willing to give governing bodies the information and space to govern.

Management, leadership and governance

Headteachers manage; headteachers and governing bodies together provide leadership, and governing bodies (with headteachers usually a member) govern.

Management involves setting up and implementing systems that enable and encourage the achievement of aims, and the collection of information that reveals how far those aims have been realised.

Leadership is about developing and communicating a vision – by word and deed – and taking important strategic decisions on key priorities.

Governance is that part of leadership which involves people who are representative of different interest groups (stakeholders) standing apart from the daily bustle of the organisation to plot a course for the future, and accounting for the organisation's use of public resources.

The Ofsted Framework illustrates what inspectors look for from the professional leadership and how it differs from their expectations of governing bodies. The descriptions below, taken from the 2009 framework, show what Ofsted would judge to be "good".

> ## Good quality management, leadership and governance
> **The effectiveness of leadership and management in embedding ambition and driving improvement**
>
> The senior leadership team and many middle leaders and managers consistently communicate high expectations to staff about securing improvement. They galvanise the enthusiasm of staff and channel their efforts to good effect. Leaders and managers conduct a range of rigorous monitoring activities relating to teaching, other provision and outcomes. Planning involves any relevant major partners and is founded on robust evidence and good-quality data. It is tackling key areas of weakness, including those in teaching, systematically and building on areas of strength. As a result teaching is at least satisfactory and improving. Consequently, outcomes are generally good, or there is substantial evidence that they are improving strongly.
>
> **The effectiveness of the governing body in challenging and supporting the school so that weaknesses are tackled decisively and statutory responsibilities met.**
>
> The governing body has the capacity to meet the school's needs and is influential in determining the strategic direction of the school. Governors are rigorous in ensuring that pupils and staff are safe and discharge their statutory duties effectively. They are fully and systematically involved in evaluating the school. Their relationships with staff are constructive and they show determination in challenging and supporting the school in tackling weaknesses and so bringing about necessary improvements. Governors have clear systems for seeking the views of parents and pupils and mechanisms for acting on these.

Governing bodies expect their headteachers to be good managers. They need to steer clear of operational management issues themselves. Otherwise they risk undermining the confidence of their headteacher, they will confuse staff and parents, and generally muddy the waters.

Governing bodies expect their headteachers also to be strong leaders in their own right, to encourage the development of leadership skills among other staff, and to value and encourage the effective leadership role of their governing body.

Headteachers need energetic and effective governing bodies that focus on the issues that will make the biggest difference to the school, and value and encourage vigorous leadership from their headteacher. Some "hero heads" may prefer a supine or comatose governing body to keep out of the way, but no amount of narcotic will keep governors permanently insensible to their powers and responsibilities. "Hero heads" cannot go on for ever but governing bodies do; and the durability of the hero's work depends on the actions of the governing body when the hero departs. In any case, no one person can be expected to do all the thinking, and even if they do most of it they need other people to bounce their ideas off. The Ofsted description of good governance says of governors "Their relationships with staff are constructive." Governors should avoid interpreting this as an invitation to become embroiled in day-to-day operations; it means that governing bodies should look for opportunities to provide material and moral support for staff efforts and should ensure that they remain well-informed about progress.

This book will provide structured practical advice to help everyone avoid strained relationships and achieve more purposeful and effective working. Everyone needs to feel that their effort is worthwhile. Governors and headteachers want these efforts to secure the best possible outcomes for all the pupils in their school.

To this end this book will address:

- how headteachers and governors can help each other perform their distinctive roles (chapter 1)
- how governors and headteachers can establish firm foundations for reciprocal working (chapter 2)
- how headteachers and governors can survive mistakes (chapter 3)
- how headteachers can give the governing body the information it needs to govern; and how governors can use that information to encourage and empower headteachers (chapter 4)
- how headteachers and governing bodies can help each other to clarify how well the school is performing (chapter 5)
- how governors can improve their headteacher's work-life balance; and how headteachers can help them meet this aim (chapter 6)
- how heads and their governing bodies can exploit the opportunities and avoid the pitfalls provided by changing relationships with national and local government (chapter 7).

IF YOU DO WHAT YOU'VE ALWAYS DONE, YOU'LL GET WHAT YOU'VE ALWAYS GOT

The advice contained in these pages implies some quite significant change for many headteachers and governors. There may be a temptation to regard it as all too much bother. You may feel that your governing body is jogging along satisfactorily (or struggling to keep up) but that no one has the time or energy to do anything extra or different. This would be a pity. Much of the advice on the following pages will not increase anyone's effort in the long term; instead it will help everyone to use their energies more productively. It should ensure that more governors feel fully involved and want to take on a bigger share of the tasks which currently often fall to headteacher and chair. Where extra work really is involved, I am confident that the benefits will far outstrip the effort required and make it well worthwhile.

Some of the difficulty in even the best-regulated governing bodies lies in what governors traditionally do. Chapter 1 argues that governors and their headteachers spend more time on some of the mechanistic aspects of governance than is now really necessary. This is one of the reasons why many governors understandably feel they cannot take on any more tasks. The answer is some radical pruning. This will allow space for more vigorous growth of the remaining tasks, allowing you to tackle key issues for the long-term future of your school and to play a much more pro-active role in communicating, consulting and involving the people your school serves.

Not everything I suggest in this book will be applicable to your school circumstances, but the principles certainly should apply and the examples, I hope, will spark your own ideas about how your governing body will work more effectively – ultimately for the benefit of your pupils and your community.

There may be a temptation to pick all the things that *other people* need to do to make *your* life easier and to reject as impractical all those things that require *you* to change. This would be to misconstrue the principle of mutuality upon which this book is based. Actually, the easiest things to change are those over which you have direct control; and if you show you are prepared to make changes, it is easier to expect others to reciprocate.

The principles upon which these ideas are constructed were learned at the feet of some of the most experienced and inspirational governor developers over the past 20 years. In particular, Joan Sallis has stressed the centrality of roles, relationships and rules. Her book, *Heads in Partnership: Working with your governors for a successful school* (Pearson, 2001) makes vital reading for aspiring, new and not-so-new headteachers. In addition, Jane Martin and Ann Holt have done much to clarify the role of the school governor in their book *Joined-up Governance* (Adamson Publishing, revised edn 2007). I am sure I have absorbed insights and phrases from many other colleagues over the years and may repeat them unconsciously in this book. I hope readers who spot them will recognise it as the sincerest form of flattery!

Note on the second edition

Since the first edition of this book was published in 2007 some important research papers have been published on the constitution and role of governing bodies. These present some significant conclusions:

A report from the University of Manchester focussing on the difficulties of governance, particularly in areas of disadvantage or with schools in special measures, suggested that the stakeholder model of governance and large governing bodies is an impediment to effective governance.

The Coalition's education White Paper, *The Importance of Teaching*, suggested smaller governing bodies were more efficient. This was followed by legislation allowing governing bodies to reconstitute, with as few as seven governors, and with less prescription on the numbers from the different categories of governor.

Developments in relation to the previous government's Every Child Matters agenda, extended services, 14-19 curriculum and leadership succession planning have all highlighted the need for increased collaboration between schools. This is reflected in the revised Ofsted framework where the quality and impact of partnership working is evaluated as a key aspect of leadership and management.

Researchers from the University of Bath (Chris James and Steve Brammer) found that while school governing is generally working well, it is "overloaded, overcomplicated and overlooked".

A report from the University of Warwick (Stewart Ranson and Colin Crouch) examined forms of cluster and locality governance developed in response to the Every Child Matters agenda, extended services, 14-19 curriculum and leadership succession planning, which all create a need for increased collaboration between schools.

Emerging models of school leadership, and specifically distributed leadership, promoted by the National College of Leadership in Schools and Children's Services, suggest that partnership working with the governing body should not be confined to the headteacher.

None of these developments have undermined the central principles of partnership between school leaders and governors. They do, however, inform the revisions to relevant parts of the text.

1. CLARIFYING THE GOVERNING BODY'S ROLES

How headteachers and governors can help each other perform their distinctive roles

When governors and headteachers are unclear about their distinctive roles it can lead to frustrations on each side: heads feeling that governing bodies take up a lot of time with little tangible result, and governors feeling that the levers for school improvement are out of their reach. And even when those levers are within reach, governors may fail to recognise and grasp them. Headteachers sometimes feel threatened when governors try to exercise a legitimate part of their role; at other times governors can become embroiled in things that are not governing body responsibilities at all.

However, an effective partnership between headteacher and governors, which enables each to carry out their different roles, is a really powerful agent for school success and is worth working to achieve.

THREE KEY ROLES

The role that governing bodies play is most commonly summarised under three headings:

- strategic decision-making
- accountability – the governing body taking responsibility for the effects of its decisions
- the "critical friend" – providing a balance of challenge and support.

Each of these will be described in turn in this chapter, and it will be demonstrated that:

- if a governing body makes effective strategic decisions it will provide the framework that frees the headteacher to lead and inspire
- if the headteacher provides a full and clear account to governors, the governing body will be able to be properly accountable to its stakeholders and help to promote the school
- if a governing body acts as an effective critical friend it will stimulate the headteacher's leadership.

1. STRATEGIC DECISION-MAKING

Strategic thinking is long-term and whole-school – even whole-community; it is reflective rather than knee-jerk, creative and innovative; it takes into account external challenges and opportunities; above all it is concerned with effectiveness. Ofsted has defined a strategic governing body as one which focuses on the quality of teaching and learning and the quality of provision. In other words governors who are more concerned with brains than drains!

The text below describes some practical ways in which governors can act strategically.

> ## Examples of being strategic
>
> ### Long-term, whole-school solutions
> A school that wants to improve its results by next year will use tactics such as deploying the best teachers to the examination classes, organising extra booster sessions, teaching to the test and cramming. Any improvements gained as a result of this are bound to level off.
>
> A strategic solution that will take longer but which will produce significant improvement over many more years will include: recruiting, retaining and developing quality staff throughout the school; focusing on really effective teaching and personalised learning; tracking progress and analysing data to identify areas for improvement; tackling poor behaviour, low-level disruption and low attendance; involving parents; striving for continuously improved inclusion.
>
> ### Whole-community
> A school with children living in disadvantaged or disorganised families may prioritise the provision of extended services and work with other agencies to remove some of the most serious barriers to children's learning and development.
>
> ### Reflective
> Inclusion issues can be treated as a long list of different groups that need to be addressed separately. A reflective approach recognises that there are common issues that can be addressed by common strategies, and these actually help everyone. For instance, travellers, looked after children, refugees and asylum seekers are all likely to arrive mid-year. By improving the school's induction processes you will help these groups and anyone else who moves into the area.
>
> ### Creative
> A school which predicts that long term demographic trends will mean fewer pupils may choose not to get into cut-throat competition with neighbouring schools but to use surplus space to establish a fully equipped training room for its own use and also to let out to other schools and organisations – having established that there would be a demand!

Strategic working by a governing body includes determining vision, aims, priorities and policies.

Sharing your vision and aims
Determining vision and aims is an occasional but essential activity for governing bodies – occasional because once agreed with a new headteacher, or revised after a period of change in circumstances or governor turnover, it should remain constant for a good length of time; essential because it should inform all decisions about priorities and policies. Vision and aims also need to be understood by stakeholders. Some governing bodies have used an INSET day for joint discussions with staff; others have set up meetings to involve staff, parents, pupils and others.

All key decisions taken by a headteacher and governing body should be consistent with the school's vision and aims. Yet many governing bodies give insufficient time to consider these and as a result fail to give their headteachers a clear mandate on how to focus the school's development. Any school will frequently experience conflicting short-term pressures and be subject to the demands of a variety of interest groups, and these can pull it in different directions.

The temptation in these circumstances is for the headteacher to decide direction and just tell the governors. This will certainly be quicker in the short term but is not in the long-term interests of the school. Partnership requires an investment of time, and if governors do not understand what they have consented to, there is every chance that they will keep arguing from positions that are inconsistent with the direction that they are supposed to have agreed on.

The vision and aims for the school, therefore, need to be thrashed out, reviewed and renewed by the governing body and headteacher together. The great strength of a governing body is that it brings together people with different perspectives – parent, staff and community. Robust argument allows these differences to be debated and resolved, by a vote if necessary. And the decision will be better understood once it has been examined from different angles, and better remembered too. As the main professional adviser to the governing body (as well as a governor in most cases) the headteacher will, of course, have a major role to play in those discussions, but it is crucial that the ultimate decision is shared. By taking strategic discussions seriously, the governing body will be helping the headteacher to be reflective when she or he comes to consider making a recommendation on some matter requiring a governing body decision.

"Governors appointed me for my vision, and now they want to discuss it!"

Selection panels for new heads invariably explore the candidates' visions for the school and seek a professional who shows a strong commitment to their vision. This does not mean that the governing body should follow their new headteacher's ideas unquestioningly. Discussion deepens understanding, tests ideas from different perspectives and in different situations, and helps to ensure the vision is robust, widely supported and sustainable. And, of course, that vision might be somewhat different when the new head has got to know the school better.

Even governing bodies and heads who want to work together on vision, aims and priorities may stumble without the tools to do it. An excellent book by David Marriott, *Being Strategic* (see page 56), provides a wealth of ideas about the "how" as well as the "what".

Sharing decisions about priorities and development plans

School development planning is still an area where many governing bodies do little more than rubber-stamp the work of the headteacher. But the plan is the blueprint for the school and must be at the heart of a governing body's work. It is crucial therefore that headteachers involve the governing body at the outline stage when priorities are being decided.

There are always more things that you could do than time or resources allow, so the plan prioritises a limited number of changes for the school to focus on. These will be the areas that governing body and headteacher agree are the most important or urgent ones. The headteacher is thus implicitly given permission to leave others on the back burner. One helpful by-product of the process is that it makes it much easier to deal with people who question why an issue they regard as important is not being dealt with immediately: "We debated this and for the following reasons decided that it was less urgent than some other issues…"

Being strategic about policies

Governing bodies spend a lot of time looking at policies, but they are not always being strategic when they do this. The list of statutorily required policies can be intimidating, and the injunction to keep policies under review can lure governing bodies into a "painting the Forth Bridge" frame of mind. Of course, schools need clear policies, but after at least three rounds of Ofsted inspection there will be few schools that do not have most of them by now (though the list of statutory policies does change).

It is also true that policies need to be reviewed to ensure they remain relevant, but some governing bodies are tempted to spend hours combing through them all in detail, to the exclusion of more important issues (see the Annex to this chapter, pages 17–19). A strategic governing body will avoid treating policies in a mechanistic way and will focus its efforts on those few that will make a real difference to the school. For example, in a school where behaviour is excellent the behaviour policy will not require attention, while in another school governors and head may feel that it is the crucial lever for improving standards. In another school, where the problem is insufficient challenge for more able pupils, governors will want to spend time looking at the policy for gifted and talented pupils. Whatever the critical area, governing bodies will be able to give it real attention if they are not bogged down with revising a lot of routine policies.

The strategic headteacher will advise the governing body on which policy areas do not require attention and those which can be dealt with perfectly adequately by headteacher and staff (with a brief report to the governing body), and will help to identify those on which governing body and headteacher need to work together. The governing body should use this advice – not uncritically – to schedule the drafting or revision of those in the last category, and then discuss the principles that it expects to see in the drafts that the headteacher and staff will produce.

Being strategic about setting the budget

Governing bodies set budgets every year, but this is not done strategically if it merely consists in an uncritical tweaking of the figures from previous years. Tighter budgets make strategic thinking more vital. Headteachers can help their governors to be more strategic by involving them in examining how their school's spending pattern compares with that of similar schools. Discovering schools which spend different proportions of their budget on, say, support staff or premises-related costs may indicate more room for manoeuvre than previously thought. Headteachers can be as frustrated as anyone by the apparent lack of options, but a governing body that helps to find more "wriggle room" will enable theirs to do things that may have seemed impossible within the funding available.

Steering clear of operational matters

The strategic governing body will help the headteacher to lead by keeping well away from operational matters. Sometimes governors may even need to resist requests from the headteacher to rule on these. At other times, a controversial operational issue will tempt one or more governors to become involved. Similar instances can arise when governors have professional knowledge of human resources, of accountancy or even of schools as Ofsted inspectors. Though these skills can be very useful, they should not be deployed to interfere in school management.

When it's OK for governors to engage with operational thinking

In limited circumstances it can be helpful to headteachers if they can discuss operational issues with governors. A headteacher may choose to use the governing body as a sounding board, especially where an operational decision such as reorganising classes or teachers may upset parents. The head can rehearse the thinking behind what they are thinking of doing and have the opportunity to hear how some representative parents and others react to it. If parents then approach governors they can be reassured that the head has thought the matter through carefully.

On a more regular basis, the headteacher should be encouraged to use the chair of governors as a sounding board. It helps the chair to better understand the headteacher's job and see how the governing body agenda fits into a bigger picture. It provides a regular opportunity for the head to be reflective and it helps to address the problem of isolation experienced by some heads.

Avoid getting enmeshed in technical detail

A discussion paper arising from the *21st Century Schools* White Paper suggested that governing bodies should stop doing some non-strategic tasks (although it did not go on to specify what might be subtracted from governing body responsibilities). We might identify what some of the items could be. We expect school management to have effective systems for safeguarding children, managing finances, reviewing teachers' pay and securing health and safety. Governing bodies are responsible for ensuring that these systems are working effectively, which requires a certain level of understanding. However, the time required to understand all the technical detail diverts governors from their strategic role. The answer is for the governing body to commission and be prepared to pay for independent expert advice in these areas and take action on any recommendations made.

Free up the headteacher by clear delegation

While the difference between operational and strategic is a useful guide, there remain some grey areas between them that have proved to be fertile ground for misunderstanding and conflict. Calls for the government to rule definitively in those areas has been sensibly resisted. However, governors and headteachers can negotiate their own arrangements. A planning tool on CD-Rom entitled *Managing the Work of the Governing Body* (see page 56) contains a useful delegation planner enabling governing bodies to decide which tasks will be retained by the full governing body and which ones will be delegated to a governing body committee, an individual or the headteacher.

A governing body that wants to make time for the strategic decisions may wish to give as many of the less significant tasks as possible to the headteacher. This does not actually add to the headteacher's work as it reduces the number of tasks where the governing body asks for their recommendation on what to do and then sends them off to do it. Instead, the headteacher completes the task and simply reports what has been done to a committee or full governing body.

By investing some time on this delegation exercise, governors (and headteachers) can obtain a clearer idea of their full responsibilities. This can be helpful in itself but, more importantly, it makes absolutely clear which tasks it has agreed to delegate and to whom.

2. ACCOUNTABILITY

Governing bodies are ultimately responsible for the quality of education provided to the children and young people in our schools; we are accountable to them and their parents. The decisions that we make as governing bodies will affect the working lives of the staff. The use of the resources (money, premises and staff) we control and the quality of future citizens which those resources help to produce is of more than passing interest to the general public. Governing bodies are therefore required to provide information and explanations to parents, pupils, staff and the wider community.

Providing accounts for stakeholders is a useful discipline for governors. It forces them to be reflective, to look back on what has been achieved and to look forward, describing agreed strategies for further improvement. The governing body's communication with pupils, parents, staff and the wider community is a very important way in which governors can support their headteacher in promoting their school. (See page 33.)

Governing bodies cannot exercise this accountability effectively unless headteachers accept and take seriously their own accountability to the governing body. A governing body which fails to call its headteacher to account might appear to reduce his or her workload but is not doing the headteacher – or the school – any favours in the long term. If governors do not know what is

Clarifying the governing body's roles

going on they are unable to provide the praise and encouragement that we all need in our work. They will not know when timescales for implementation have slipped or changes have failed to bring the desired improvement, and are therefore unable to urge corrective action until problems become obvious to outsiders. They will not have the deep and thorough understanding of the school that is essential if they are to contribute to the most important strategic decisions.

The headteacher's accountability to the governing body is expressed most obviously in the headteacher's report, which is discussed in more detail in chapter 4. The discipline of preparing it encourages headteachers to lift their thoughts away from the day-to-day concerns, to be reflective, and to look both back and forwards.

For more detail on this role, read Stephen Adamson's *Accountability: A practical guide for school governors* (see page 56).

3. THE "CRITICAL FRIEND"

"Critical friend" has become the accepted way of summarising the governing body's role of challenge and support. Those who feel uncomfortable with the word "critical" have been reminded that a film critic can describe a performance as "stupendous"; but even when governors need to say "surely we can do better than this" they say it in the context of "friends" who want the best for the school and its students. After all, it is only your best friend (or children!) who can be relied on to tell you the unpalatable truth. So a governing body needs to recognise and celebrate what the school does well, and it needs to know where the school is not achieving as well as it could. The critical friend governing body, however, is not just a bystander but enters wholeheartedly – at the strategic level – in discussions about strategies for improvement, offering encouragement and the benefit of wider experience where appropriate.

The balance between challenge and support has been illustrated in the then DfES's *Governing the School of the Future* (2004) by the diagram below.

High support

Supporters club	Partners or "critical friends"
"We're here to support the head"	*"We share everything – good or bad"*

Low challenge ———————————————— **High challenge**

Abdicators	Adversaries
"We leave it to the professionals"	*"We keep a very close eye on the staff"*

Low support

Since honest self-evaluation is the best way to begin any improvement, you might like to reflect on where your governing body (not individuals) is within this matrix. What do you think would help the governing body to move closer to the top right corner?

The critical friend role comes into play both in strategic decision-making and receiving headteachers' accounts. For instance, a governing body might challenge a policy recommendation which the headteacher would prefer to go through on the nod. This can actually be very supportive if it improves the decision or increases governors' understanding of a difficult issue. It may be that following "challenging" discussion, the headteacher's recommendation is agreed. When parents or staff ask why the decision was taken, governors will not respond, "Because our head told us," – that's no support at all – but head and governors can say together, "We looked at this issue very carefully and for the following reasons we concluded that this was the best way forward – or the least worst option."

Challenge and support are both appropriate responses to any account provided by the headteacher. Governors will be able to see and praise achievements and targets met. They may receive reports of slippages in timescales or targets not met. Here the appropriate response will be to question why, and listen – sympathetically but critically – to the answers given. Being adversarial and casting around for someone to blame is only likely to engender anxiety and defensiveness. On the other hand, the laissez-faire or supporters' club approach of letting things like this go without comment is of no help to anybody.

Sympathetic probing may reveal that the timescales were unrealistic, insufficient resources were available to achieve them or the targets were too high; in all these instances there are learning points for everyone. It may be that circumstances such as staff illness have blown an initiative off course, in which case it is appropriate to ask what a realistic new timescale would be.

Headteachers can discourage governors from carrying out their critical friend role if they respond in an offended and defensive manner whenever they are challenged. On the other hand, they can encourage their governing body to develop and refine its critical friend skills by welcoming challenge even when it is couched in clumsy language. They may also need to remind governors about offering praise and encouragement to staff while providing the prompts by telling them of staff achievements. As educationalists, inculcating positive attitudes and good habits should not be too difficult – and, of course, modelling behaviours is a powerful strategy.

EFFECTIVE HEADTEACHERS	EFFECTIVE GOVERNING BODIES
Manage the school effectively.	Keep away from operational matters.
Share the leadership role with their governing body.	Share the leadership role with their headteacher.
Advise governors about key strategic issues.	Focus on key strategic issues.
Assist in high-quality discussion with the governing body to jointly arrive at vision, aims and objectives.	Make time for high-quality discussion with the headteacher to jointly arrive at vision, aims and objectives.
Accept as many delegated tasks as they can handle.	Delegate non-strategic tasks to their headteacher where possible.
Provide the information that the governing body needs so it can be properly accountable.	Provide information and explanations to parents, pupils, staff and others and ensure the governing body is properly accountable.
Encourage their governing body to ask challenging questions.	Aren't afraid to ask challenging questions.
Provide governors with information that gives opportunities to praise.	Seek out and use opportunities to celebrate progress and achievement.

ANNEX: SOME STRATEGIC CHALLENGES FOR GOVERNING BODIES

The preceding chapter has suggested that headteachers and governing bodies should make time for thorough consideration of key strategic challenges. This annex suggests what some of these challenges are likely to be.

Making resources go further ...

Governing bodies will have to get used to being expected to deliver more with stand-still budgets and with potentially less support from cash-strapped local authorities. This will increase the importance of taking a hard look at historic spending patterns and building on workforce remodelling to restructure staffing. It may also involve collaborating with other schools to share staff such as bursars, technicians and subject specialists, to purchase more economically in bulk and to offer a wider range of extra-curricular activities.

It is not only budget constraints that call for the careful husbanding of resources. Schools use energy and can both teach and model environmental responsibility. Governing bodies will need to consider how they can involve the whole school community in efforts to reduce their school's carbon footprint.

As the role and resources of the local authority shrink, governing bodies need to work together to ensure that the local government activities that really help schools are retained – probably funded by contributions from school budgets. Governing bodies and school leaders will need to develop their skills in commissioning and subsequently evaluating high-quality, good-value services from providers, whether local authority or outside consultants.

... and making better use of volunteers

Despite the uncertainties planted in many people's minds by the vetting and barring scheme, volunteers should be a real help. The increasing number of retired and semi-retired people with health, time and energy constitute a growing resource available to schools. Schools, particularly those developing extended services, can provide a myriad of structured volunteering opportunities. Governing bodies can help other school leaders to bring fresh thinking and identify all the volunteering opportunities that already exist and others that can be further developed. They can have an advocacy role in advertising their schools' need for volunteers among parents, friends and the wider community.

Addressing pupil wellbeing

Since the 2004 Children Act governing bodies and school leaders have become increasingly adept in tackling the question of pupil wellbeing at school level:

- tightening safeguarding procedures
- promoting healthy eating and active lifestyles
- developing enjoyable and challenging learning experiences
- listening and responding to pupil concerns and ideas
- improving attendance and promoting enterprise and other work-related skills.

Despite this, few schools can claim that all children are achieving all the outcomes as well as they could. The inexorable growth of sedentary screen-based activity, continuing trends in obesity, examples of anti-social behaviour, bullying, risky behaviours (including in the use of the internet) and the disengagement of significant numbers of young people and families mean that much remains to be done. Narrowing the gap in academic performance and well-being remains a huge challenge across the country. Identifying the barriers that prevent some groups reaping the benefits of all that schools offer and straining every sinew to dismantle those impediments is a key strategic task that all schools should take up. Often the solutions are likely to involve parents and carers, especially those who are "hard to reach".

This is the extended services agenda, of course. Progress again often involves working collaboratively with other schools, agencies and voluntary bodies and developing more effective two-way communication with parents and other members of the local community. The next phase in the development of Children's Trusts will require a much closer relationship so that strategic decisions taken by the Trusts are informed by the work of schools and strongly support their schools. The strategic governing body will engage in discussions with other schools and agencies to determine locally how this can best be achieved.

Reforms to the curriculum

At the time of revising this text major changes were underway in the National Curriculum. These will be implemented in 2014 and will affect the teaching of all the core subjects in both primary and secondary schools.

However, the curriculum is much more than the contents of the National Curriculum, or even the subjects taught. Governing bodies need to avoid being sucked too quickly into discussion about "subjects", where many governors are not well qualified to contribute. The strategic governing body will focus on broader principles about the sort of people we want our education system to develop.

Making a contribution to community cohesion

Schools have been called upon to play a key part in a developing harmony nationally through their duty to promote community cohesion. Real understanding of different cultures and religions is an essential foundation for the building of social cohesion in a diverse society.

Making workforce remodelling work for your school

Research conducted by London Metropolitan University in August 2009 (*Workforce Remodelling: Strategies used and impact on workload and standards,* www.dcsf.gov.uk – search "remodelling strategies") suggests a mixed picture of the impact so far of the national agreement on workload and standards. At least part of the problem seems to be that many schools have seen compliance with statutory requirements as the aim rather than seeking to understand key principles and actively consulting and involving staff in finding solutions appropriate to the school. This is an area that governing bodies could grasp as a key strategic task. There are many case studies on the Training and Development Agency (TDA) website, www.tda.gov.uk/remodelling/managingchange/resources, that schools can learn from.

Governing bodies can work in partnership with headteachers to:

- develop, use and pay appropriately, Higher Level Teacher Assistants (HLTAs)
- identify further scope for transferring complex administrative or pastoral roles to support staff
- review the current staffing structure and ask whether it is really the most effective way to achieve the school's aims
- bring a member of support staff into the senior leadership team
- check workload and stress on administrative staff
- ensure that there is appropriate space in school for PPA time and that it is timetabled in useful blocks to allow planning with colleagues
- be realistic about the workload implications of providing extended services and find ways to deploy funds and staffing accordingly
- survey the perceptions of staff as well as receiving reports from the headteacher
- explain the expected benefits of proposed changes to staff and parents.

Making extended services work for your community

Much has already been achieved in providing or signposting a wide range of extended services. The strategic issues that need to be addressed by governing bodies in the coming years include:

- sustaining extended services as budgets are squeezed

- ensuring that disadvantaged young people are encouraged and enabled to take part in a wide range of activities
- constructing robust decision-making and accountability mechanisms to enable the most effective use of funds allocated to clusters of schools.

Making plans to secure effective leadership for years to come

Concern over the number of headteachers coming to the end of their working lives in the next decade is stimulating new thinking about leadership from the National College for Leadership in Schools and Children's Services. Governing bodies need to be active partners in:

- identifying and developing leadership talent throughout their schools
- encouraging the development of distributed leadership which replaces the need to have perfect leaders with the more practical proposition of building perfect teams
- helping staff to have a better understanding of partnership with the governing body
- preparing and encouraging appropriate staff to become headteachers
- finding ways to retain effective headteachers – for example, by encouraging them to take up fresh challenges such as being a School Improvement Partner, or enabling them to ease into retirement with a part-time co-headship, or building a fulfilling partnership that any leader would be loath to leave!
- being ready to offer support from your headteacher and other staff to a struggling school
- establishing collaborative arrangements with other schools to share some of the burdens of headship
- being open to the possibility that collaborative arrangements might evolve into fully fledged federation, if that is the best way to secure the most effective education for the children and young people in your community.

The National College has produced an excellent toolkit for governors at www.nationalcollege.org.uk – search "Toolkit for Governors".

Making your buildings fit for learning in the 21st century

Government funding for Building Schools for the Future, and its primary equivalent the Primary Capital Programme, gives governing bodies an opportunity and a responsibility to work with their headteacher and the local authority in identifying needs in the area and defining an education vision and long-term strategy for the school and its community. Governors will want to find ways of involving young people in these discussions and decisions.

2. PRINCIPLES OF PARTNERSHIP

How headteachers and governors can establish a firm foundation for reciprocal working

The previous chapter focused on what governing bodies and headteachers do and how they can assist each other in their distinctive roles. This chapter will consider the *attitudes* and *values* that form the foundation for effective partnership working.

Mutual respect comes from the recognition of important and distinctive roles (as described in chapter 1) and mutual appreciation of the professional skills of the headteacher and the breadth of experience and common sense of governors.

Headteachers and governors often avoid argument fearing it may damage relationships, but the free exchange of views is vital to a democratic forum. The eighteenth-century Scottish philosopher, David Hume, once said, "Truth springs from argument among friends." Governing bodies have quite deliberately been made up from people who bring different perspectives – parent, staff and wider community – with the intention that those differences would be aired and better decisions result. The important thing to remember is "argument *among friends*"; we all want the best for children and we listen to and engage with those different points of view.

Mutual respect should also translate into mutual support. Governing bodies which keep asking themselves, "How is our action helping our headteacher?" Headteachers who ask themselves, "How can I help my governing body to work more effectively to help me do my job?" Sceptical heads who are not sure why they should bother, are advised to refer back to the Introduction (pages 5–6) to remind themselves of the importance that Ofsted now places on governance. Effective governing bodies can help heads to be more strategic; ineffective governing bodies can use up and sometimes drain time and energy. It is therefore sensible for heads to invest time in helping their governing body to be effective, and governors need to put commitment and effort into improving their effectiveness to enable the headteacher's leadership to flourish.

Partnership involves sharing a vision of where we are going. Chapter 1 argued that headteachers and governing bodies should share the development of the vision for the school. At a more prosaic level the headteacher and all governors should have a clear understanding of the schedule of work for the year. This helps to keep everyone focused on the tasks that will really make a difference and makes it easier to collect information needed to carry out each task effectively.

Partnership involves sharing information which is essential for a common understanding of issues and options. Headteachers have most of the information about the school and, as already mentioned, the governing body cannot be genuinely accountable without it. But governors also have information that they glean as the "eyes and ears" outside the school; this too needs to be shared as part of the school's self-evaluation.

Partners share ideas. Mutual respect implies that everyone has ideas to contribute. So, while it respects the professionalism of headteacher and staff, the governing body may have different ideas because it has a different perspective. The best ideas rarely emerge fully formed and governing bodies may need to develop skills to recognise the kernel of a great idea in an "off-the-wall" suggestion from the most naive individual.

Partnership involves sharing responsibility. In terms of governing body work there is no way to avoid the legal fact that the governing body is responsible for everything done in its name, even if delegated. All governors (including, of course, the head as a governor) abide by, explain and justify governing body decisions. This underlines the importance of headteachers ensuring that governors understand the reasons for difficult decisions. Unless governors take time to understand why a decision is being recommended – and why alternative options are less satisfactory – they cannot effectively support their headteacher by justifying the decision.

Partners share the work. Of course, headteachers are full-time professionals and governors are very part-time volunteers so it is not reasonable to expect equal work; but there is an expectation that governors will pull their weight. Governors who expect the headteacher to lead the governing body and do all the hard work cannot expect to be regarded as real partners. There is a lesson here also for individual governors who must accept their share of the work. If everything is left to the chair or a small group of governors the governing body cannot function effectively.

Partnership involves sharing the credit. Governors are usually happy to let the headteacher and staff take the credit for school successes. After all, they are at the sharp end in delivering high-quality education. But everyone needs encouragement and recognition, and a governing body that has basked in a little glory will be better motivated to develop their role.

Trust is a vital ingredient in partnership: it frees up headteachers to get on with the job without feeling that governors are breathing down their neck on every issue, and it brings governors into discussions on difficult issues at an early stage. There is (often) a temptation to say, "Let's not worry them about this until we've sorted it out in our own minds and can make a recommendation." In some cases this may be appropriate but it is not always the most sensible view. The leadership team may not find time to do the thinking until the issue has become urgent and then may take rushed decisions. Discussing the issue with the governing body earlier might have forced the reflective thinking that helps ensure strong decisions. The expertise and experience of individuals on the governing body could have helped the thinking. Worse still is where governors get to hear about something that they feel has been withheld from them. This undermines trust.

Trust has to be earned. By sharing information – good and bad – a headteacher can demonstrate and earn trust. By treating sensitive information in confidence, avoiding the temptation to jump to conclusions or to seek to pin blame rather than explore lessons, governing bodies can gain the confidence of their head. The individual governor who leaks information can spoil it for everyone else; so regular reminders about confidentiality and concerted peer group pressure on any transgressions are very important.

COMPLAINTS AND GRIEVANCES

Governors can sometimes find themselves dragged inappropriately into parental complaints or staff grievances. Dealing with these should almost always be an internal school matter which may be resolved before it reaches the head or will be sorted by the headteacher. This is why it is essential that a governing body needs to be sure that the school has an approved complaints procedure which is known to parents and a grievance procedure known to all staff.

The governing body should only become involved if the headteacher has failed to resolve an issue to the satisfaction of the complainant who then takes it to the governing body – and then, of course, it will only be a small number of governors, typically three, who form a panel to hear the complaint or grievance. (See chapter 3.)

PARTNERSHIP BETWEEN HEADTEACHER AND CHAIR OF GOVERNORS

The relationship between headteacher and chair is of vital importance in the effective operation of any governing body. As leader and representative of the governing body the chair should aim to epitomise and model the attitudes and values described in this chapter. This involves working with the headteacher and other governors to:

- Plan and organise the work of the governing body by:
    - drawing up a schedule of work for the year to ensure that all the important tasks are spread appropriately across the year – with some space to deal with the unexpected
    - ensuring a sufficient number (not too many) of committees with clear terms of reference derived from the delegation decisions described on page 14
    - ensuring strong and committed membership of each committee
    - agreeing dates for all full governing body and committee meetings for the year.
- Share those plans with all other governors to develop understanding and commitment.
- Share out the work between meetings to underline corporate responsibility. For example, most communications sent to the chair of governors are not restricted to the chair and should be passed around for different governors to deal with as necessary.
- Chase progress between meetings (jointly undertaken with a good clerk). There are few things more frustrating to headteachers and other governors than learning that an agreed action has stalled because of poor follow-up. Regular discussion with the head can ensure that school staff are on track, while communication with chairs of committees and other individual governors where appropriate can ensure that governors do not let the side down.
- Plan an effective agenda for each meeting, giving appropriate notice and supplying necessary papers. This, of course, will involve close working with the clerk.
- Consider succession planning. One of the more unsettling problems for a headteacher may be when a long-established chair steps down and no governor is willing to take over. Sharing the work and developing governor skills through training and practice in chairing committees are key elements in succession planning. Chair and head must avoid any suggestion of a stitch-up so it is important that as many governors as possible are given opportunities to develop. Useful guidance on this, *Succession Breeds Success*, produced by a group of governor service managers, can be found on the NCOGS website www.ncogs.org.uk – look under Resources.

These tasks are all routine. There will be occasions, however, when the chair has to resolve difficulties and misunderstandings between the headteacher and other governors. In these cases a reminder about the principles of partnership and the corporate nature of governor authority may need to be set out forcefully by the chair so as to avoid the debilitating effect of a messy dispute.

In cases of difficulty with parents or staff the chair of governor's role is more in the nature of a sounding board for the headteacher. As we have seen, it should be the headteacher who sorts these difficulties out, short of the matter going to the complaints or grievances panel. Many headteachers find it useful to clarify the issues and rehearse their proposed action with the chair. This is helpful and appropriate provided that the headteacher makes the final decision and the chair is not part of any subsequent complaint or grievance process. Some governing bodies insert in their complaints policy an informal opportunity to resolve difficulties before it reaches a governor panel. The chair may be the appropriate person to get complainant and headteacher together for this purpose, provided, again, that the chair is not to be subsequently involved if resolution is not achieved.

One of the most important aspects of the relationship between the head and chair is the governing body's responsibility for the head's work-life balance. The issues surrounding this and the chair's specific role are the subject of chapter 6.

Note that nothing in this section should be construed as meaning that the chair has more powers than any other governor. The corporate nature of governance requires that, except in a real emergency, chairs should not exercise powers unless they have specifically been delegated.

PARTNERSHIP BETWEEN HEADTEACHER, CHAIR OF GOVERNORS AND THE CLERK

A good clerk is essential to an effective operation of the governing body. The clerk must be much more than a taker of minutes – although speedily produced and accurate minutes are very important. The clerk should act as an officer of the governing body to:

- offer advice when appropriate on the meaning of regulations to ensure that the governing body keeps to the straight and narrow
- advise the chair and headteacher in preparing the agenda for a governing body meeting
- chase up reports, committee minutes and other papers so that they can be sent out seven days before the meeting.

EFFECTIVE HEADTEACHERS	EFFECTIVE GOVERNING BODIES
Understand and respect the governing body role.	Respect the headteacher's professional role.
Act as professional adviser to the governing body.	
Ask how they can help their governing body.	Ask how their actions are helping the headteacher
Aren't afraid of "argument among friends".	Aren't afraid of "argument among friends".
Share information – good and bad – as soon as possible.	Avoid jumping to conclusions and apportioning blame.
	Guard confidentiality with their life!
Are prepared to address "off-the-wall" questions and ideas as learning opportunities.	Are prepared to learn from consideration of "off-the-wall" questions and ideas.
Share responsibility.	Share responsibility.
Deal with parent and staff concerns appropriately.	Direct parents and staff to appropriate channels for complaints and grievances – and only deal with them (as a panel) as the last stage of the agreed procedure.
	Share work across the governing body.

3. LEADERSHIP, GOVERNANCE AND FALLIBILITY
How headteachers and governors can survive mistakes!

We all make mistakes. The trick in any organisation is to respond to mistakes in ways that develop learning and build confidence. In learning organisations it is particularly sad when fallibility can be hard to acknowledge and mistakes made by either governors or headteachers undermine painstakingly built relationships and constructive partnerships. This chapter seeks to put mistakes in their proper perspective and set headteachers and governors free from the tyranny of blame.

Of course, organisations are right to expect high standards, and notice when things go wrong. However, both headteachers and their governing bodies should seek to establish a culture which is more forgiving of errors, which accepts that the group or its individual members sometimes get it wrong, and helps to model an ethos where headteachers and their staff are open to the possibility that they too are not infallible. Encouraging a "no blame" culture enables schools to be more creative and flexible in responding to change. Organisations that are quick to punish mistakes encourage their staff to act defensively and waste time in "covering their backs".

So, respecting the professionalism of headteachers does not require governors to think their head is always right. Judges can make mistakes, which is why the law allows appeals to a higher court. Politicians misjudge the mood of their electorate and get decisions wrong, which is why we have opposition parties. So why are some headteachers so sensitive to the suggestion that they may have made a mistake?

DEALING WITH APPEALS AND COMPLAINTS

This is most clearly illustrated when governing bodies have to adjudicate on pupil exclusions, parental complaints or staff grievances. Clearly, the fact that governing bodies have been given the legal responsibility to deal with these cases is an acceptance that sometimes things go wrong. The governor panels which are set up to hear these cases must listen to and weigh the evidence and arguments on both sides before reaching their judgement "without fear or favour". They must have regard to the principles of natural justice (see box overleaf) and there has to be a possibility that the panel will overturn their headteacher's decision or uphold a complaint. Many parents will say, "There's no point appealing or making a complaint because governors always side with the headteacher," so it is all the more important that parents (or staff) are made to feel that their case has been heard and considered carefully.

Headteachers may sometimes feel that a panel has bent over backwards to be fair to parents, and has made the wrong judgement. Particularly in the case of an overturned exclusion, the consequences of this can be very difficult to manage. There are often grey areas where a decision

> **Principles of natural justice**
>
> All parties should have adequate notice of proceedings.
>
> There should be no undue delay.
>
> Parties have the right to bring a friend.
>
> The presentation of the case should be fair to all parties.
>
> All parties should see the evidence of the other side so that they have an opportunity to prepare their case.
>
> Decisions to admit or exclude evidence should be based on whether it is relevant, reliable and logically valid.
>
> Panels should avoid hearing one side in the absence of the other party.
>
> Each party should have the opportunity to state their case adequately.
>
> Each party is entitled to ask questions and contradict the evidence of the opposing party.
>
> Panel members should declare any personal interest they may have in the proceedings.
>
> Panel members should be unbiased and act in good faith.
>
> Panel members should not judge the case until they have heard all the evidence.
>
> Panel members should take into account relevant considerations and extenuating circumstances, and ignore irrelevant considerations.
>
> Appropriate levels of confidentiality must be maintained.

could go either way, and sometimes a panel will make a mistake – they are fallible too. In those cases headteachers face the challenge both of overcoming their own disappointment, reminding staff that the panel's decision is final and finding ways to manage the implications. In these circumstances governors would expect their headteacher to explain privately and quietly to the panel members why the decision was a disappointment to them, and to avoid an unproductive public slanging match.

Mistakes are (usually) not hanging offences! Some headteachers have been known to insist that governors' consideration of a parental complaint be seen as a judgement of their own competence. This puts undue pressure on the panel and is potentially dangerous for the head. Instead, it is better to see parental complaints as a way of understanding different perceptions of the service the school provides – sometimes revealing the need for better presentation or explanation of what the school's leadership does, sometimes helping the leadership see how it can improve what it does.

A pitfall that some complaints panels fall into is to exceed their brief and inadvertently make policy. It may be clear to them – and on reflection also to the head – that the school's current procedure should be changed to avoid any repetition. But it is a mistake for the panel then to write into the judgement changes that they expect to see. Their brief was to hear and judge the complaint and they do not have delegated powers to make policy. What a panel should say in this situation is that the headteacher or governing body will be expected to review the procedure. That allows panel members to explain what they think the changes should involve, and it also allows the head and other governors to explain why their idea may not work and to devise a better solution.

When the headteacher's recommendation is not endorsed

There are other areas of potential conflict, less clear but perhaps more frequent. Recommendations made by a headteacher after long and careful consultation may not always meet with the approval of the governing body. If the governing body is acting in its proper "critical friend" role it will not allow itself to be a rubber stamp but will consider the proposal from all angles, and may prefer a different option. The problem might have been avoided if governors had been involved in some of the thinking at an earlier stage before the school leadership team had invested time and energy in developing it. It may be that insufficient preparatory work had been done to explain to governors the principles underlying the proposal. Whatever the reason, the refusal of a governing body to endorse a proposal made by the headteacher can be very discouraging. This is why some governors are tempted to accept such proposals against their better judgement. But it does the school and headteacher no favours if the proposal subsequently runs into difficulties. History books relate that there were people in Philip II of Spain's retinue who could have told him the Armada invasion of England wouldn't work, but they were afraid to speak up!

If partnership is to really work, head and governors need to build strong relationships where they can develop proposals together and feel satisfied with the outcome of their discussion – even if the decision was not as some had initially hoped.

Taking care over governor behaviour

Governing body monitoring and evaluation may reveal flaws: decisions not yet implemented or targets not met. A more serious failure may happen in the governing body's reaction to such information – carping criticism or refusal to accept the explanation proffered. A blame culture like this encourages the headteacher to become defensive and reluctant to agree challenging targets. But if governors appreciate that circumstances can blow a plan off course or delay the implementation of a decision, the school can rectify the situation and learn from the experience. Moreover, an ambitious target just missed can be a more glorious achievement than a comfortable one exceeded.

Governors (especially those with business backgrounds or whose own children are suffering) can become very impatient with what they perceive to be slow processes for tackling teacher capability, and may appear to challenge or undermine the efforts of the leadership team on this issue. A watched pot never boils; governors who breathe down the neck of their headteacher on a capability issue may inadvertently slow the process down or cause it to break down completely. So governors must not get involved unless the issue goes to appeal.

Sometimes fallibility lies in the clumsy way we express ourselves. If we all waited to compose the most carefully crafted question or comment before opening our mouths, governing body meetings would go on for months! People say things they might regret in the heat of the moment or through tiredness or frustration. Forgiveness and reminding each other that we have a common purpose (for the children's benefit) are the antidotes to such potential poison.

Sometimes a governor will upset the headteacher and staff by some instance of inappropriate behaviour in school or by letting slip confidential information. In those cases hurt and disappointment are usually more powerful weapons for headteachers to wield than anger. Anger invites defensiveness and excuses; disappointment will more readily elicit apology. Peer group pressure exerted by other governors is the best way to avoid repetition; but this depends on governors putting their reserve to one side to leave the perpetrator in no doubt about how their colleagues feel – the possible consequences of the indiscretion and the shared responsibility for building trust and maintaining partnership. "So what have we all learned? And what are we going to do about it?"

KEEPING A SENSE OF PERSPECTIVE

Sometimes it can be difficult to let go when governing body and headteacher reach an impasse. On those occasions it is instructive to think of the Sumatran monkey trap: to catch a monkey a banana is put in a narrow-necked pot. The monkey reaches through the neck to grab the banana and is then trapped because it won't let go of the bait. Sometimes headteachers or their governors won't let go even when any rational observer can see that the consequences of hanging on are going to be disastrous.

If we can all accept that we make mistakes and treat them as learning experiences it can enable us to be more effective in future. If we can forgive transgressions, make allowances for clumsiness and irritability and persist in open communication that continually builds and maintain relationships, schools will be better places in which to work, headship will remain exciting, governing will be more rewarding and, most importantly, our pupils will be better served.

EFFECTIVE HEADTEACHERS	EFFECTIVE GOVERNING BODIES
Accept that everyone makes mistakes.	Accept that everyone makes mistakes.
Encourage a "no-blame" culture among staff.	Adopt a "no-blame" approach to the headteacher.
Are forgiving of clumsiness in expression.	Avoid strong expressions of impatience when the headteacher is following set procedures.
Express disappointment rather than anger when referring to transgressions.	Express disappointment rather than anger when referring to transgressions.
Understand that governor appeal panels sometimes find against the head.	Ensure that appeal panels hear and weigh evidence from both sides "without fear or favour".
Remember that panels make decisions "on the balance of probability" rather than "beyond reasonable doubt".	Remember that panels make decisions "on the balance of probability" rather than "beyond reasonable doubt".
Take care when expressing their views about decisions that go against them.	Take care in handling the headteacher's disappointment when the decision goes against them.
Are ready to let go.	Are ready to let go.

4. REPORTING/ACCOUNTING TO THE GOVERNING BODY

How headteachers can give reports that help governors to govern, and how governors can use reports to help headteachers to lead

This chapter might have been entitled "The Headteacher's Report" but there are good reasons why it isn't.

First, we have all got into the habit of thinking that the headteacher's report is a statutory requirement; this means that some headteachers and governors treat their headteacher's report as a routine document and make insufficient use of it. But the law does not refer to the headteacher's report anywhere. This does not mean, however, that the headteacher is under no legal obligation to give the governing body information. What *A Guide to the Law for School Governors* states is:

> A good headteacher will discuss all the main aspects of school life with the governing body and will expect the governing body to both challenge and support the school ... Governors should not be deterred from questioning proposals and seeking further information to enable them to make sound decisions ..."

> The headteacher should give the governing body enough information to enable it to feel confident that both it and the headteacher are fulfilling their statutory responsibilities.

> To assist the governing body in carrying out its functions, the headteacher has a duty to provide the governing body with such reports in connection with his or her functions, as the governing body requires.

Secondly, the apostrophe may give a misleading impression of who owns the report. The extracts quoted above suggest that while much of the information will be compiled by the headteacher, it is provided for and at the behest of the governing body. This is not being pedantic; and indeed clarifying the point should be helpful both to headteacher and governing body. It means that the governing body needs to decide in partnership with their headteacher the reports that will be most useful. If the governing body has adopted the suggestions made in earlier chapters about planning ahead for the year, many of the reports will spring from that. Headteachers can focus their reporting on the issues that the governing body has agreed are most important, and can expect, therefore, that governors will make the best use of the information they have asked for.

Thirdly, committees and individual governors with delegated powers, and working parties established to investigate an issue, must also report to the governing body. Governors, too, have an important responsibility to provide clear reports; without them governing body work can become bogged down – to the frustration of heads and governors alike.

QUALITY REPORTS ARE A GOOD INVESTMENT

Recognising that the production of reports involves a lot of hard work by headteachers, it is worth remembering the rewards for conscientious reporting and considering how an effective governing body can maximise those rewards. The most important benefit of a good report is that its production requires reflection which in turn clarifies strategic thinking. It pulls together various sorts of data, adds analysis and provides a clear narrative. The result should be a better informed governing body, better able to understand what is going on in the school and therefore to make crisper strategic decisions.

CLARIFYING THE PURPOSE OF REPORTS

There are five main purposes behind reporting:

- To report what has been done using delegated powers – remember, the governing body remains responsible for the actions of the headteacher (and any other governor) under delegated powers.
- To provide information needed for making decisions – this has been described in chapter 1.
- To provide monitoring information – the implementation of decisions, policies and plans.
- To provide evaluation information – have the decisions, policies and plans worked as the headteacher and governing body expected?
- To give background information – information that is not covered by any other category but is *explicitly* relevant to future governing body decisions.

> **Everything else**
>
> There is a further category of information that comes to governors: that is Everything Else. This often swamps the really important information in headteacher reports. Governors do not know what to do with it. It has been described as "a thousand answers looking for a question"!
>
> If governors and headteachers can be proactive and work together to determine what the governing body needs, they can reduce this unfocussed and wasteful material. In providing information to the governing body – whether as headteacher, chair or other governor – it is helpful to ask, "Has the governing body requested this information (and what does it want to do with it)?" If the answer is "no", the next question to ask is "What do I want the governing body to do with this information?" If the answer is "I don't know," leave it out!

MONITORING INFORMATION

Governing bodies need to know that their decisions have been implemented, or to be told if some obstacle has got in the way. The headteacher's report or committee minutes might contain that information, if necessary, with a "Where do we go from here?" statement or recommendation. That is monitoring information.

Governors are most likely to be interested in monitoring progress on the School Development or Improvement Plan since this is the key strategic document. They will need to ensure that school spending is broadly in line with the agreed budget since significant overspend creates future difficulties and major underspend deprives students of the resources allocated for their learning.

Monitoring information provides the ammunition for governors to say "Well done" and "Thank you" – the under-used pat on the back that can help propel headteachers and staff forwards.

Monitoring the quality of teaching and learning

The quality of teaching and learning is central to a school's effectiveness, and governors are often unsure about how they can show their interest in it. They know that they are not inspectors and do not have the professional competence or the jurisdiction to make judgements in this area, but they also appreciate that this cannot justify collective ignorance. The sample report shown in the box on the next page illustrates how a headteacher can keep governors informed about the leadership team's monitoring of teaching and learning.

Governors need to know that there is a robust system for monitoring quality. They also need to know that monitoring is happening because there can be all sorts of reasons why a procedure may not be implemented properly. They will be concerned to know what the overall quality of teaching and learning is judged to be – and how it has changed over recent years. They will not be allowed to discuss individual members of staff since issues of capability need to be addressed by headteacher and senior colleagues without interference from governors; they may, however, want to satisfy themselves that there are clear processes for addressing capability issues and that the headteacher is confident in applying them.

The list of strengths and areas for development described in the sample report shows the level of analysis undertaken by the leadership team and provides information about some issues that have shown improvement and how the school proposes to develop further.

EVALUATION INFORMATION

Governing bodies also need to know whether a decision or policy is working in the way that it intended; and, more generally, what are the school's strengths and areas for improvement.

Governors will usually focus their evaluation on the effect of strategic decisions taken in earlier School Development Plans. While monitoring is relatively short-term, evaluation takes place at the end and in many cases considerably later than the implementation phase.

The best way to judge whether a decision is working in the way that you intended is to go back to the information on which you formed the decision. In many cases it should include a statement about the likely impact. "If we carry on as we are (with current pupils moving through the school) we can expect X% of pupils to attain level Y in year A; if we were to adopt this option, we would expect attainment to rise (or fall) to Z% at level Y in year A."

This gives a clue to when the evaluation information on this particular decision should be provided. In the autumn of year A the percentage of pupils gaining level Y will be known and should be compared with the prediction.

It would be naive to suppose that there will not be other factors affecting those pupils over a long period of time, and these might affect the eventual outcome. However, the statement of anticipated impact can help to focus discussion at the decision-making stage and can help the governors and headteacher learn from what happened when they come to perform an evaluation.

Effective school self-evaluation

Ofsted now expects headteachers and governors to be competent at school self-evaluation. That is why Ofsted inspection now focuses on how well the school knows itself. This is the subject of the next chapter.

Example of a headteacher's report on the quality of teaching and learning

Our leadership monitoring policy

All teachers are observed by headteacher and/or member of the leadership team on a regular basis as part of the Performance Management process. Some of these are joint observations with the SIP to ensure consistency of judgements.

Teachers' planning and children's work are also reviewed by members of the leadership team (and by subject coordinators on a rolling programme to ensure coverage across the curriculum).

Feedback is given to individual staff members as soon after lesson observation as possible and where necessary individual support and training needs are identified.

The leadership team discuss the overall findings and share key strengths and areas for development with staff at our regular staff meetings.

Analysis of results

Over the past six months the head and leadership team have observed 15 lessons. 93% of them were satisfactory or better. 56% were good or better and 14% were outstanding. One lesson (7%) was unsatisfactory. This is a slight improvement on my previous report.

Main strengths

All staff have clear objectives shared with pupils at the start of the lesson and reviewed at the end. This is an issue that we have worked on over the past year and it is now being applied consistently.

All teachers and support staff demonstrate confidence in teaching Literacy, Numeracy and Science.

All staff exhibit high expectations of pupils, and this is evident both in lessons and in the marking of children's work.

There is good differentiation with a range of challenging activities for all abilities.

There is evidence of much improved teacher subject knowledge in Religious Education. The RE Coordinator led an excellent staff meeting on planning last June and reports clear planning and good coverage in recent months.

Areas for development

Pupils are not yet as clear as they should be about their personal targets. The work we did on our training day at the beginning of term will take a little longer to bear fruit.

More practice is needed to refine and target questioning techniques.

Some staff use marking effectively to direct children to the next steps in their learning, and this needs to be applied consistently across the school. A staff meeting with a visiting Advanced Skills Teacher is planned next month.

I would like teachers to plan more activities to take maximum advantage of the highly skilled teaching assistants we now have in our school. This was discussed at a full staff meeting last week and an action plan has been agreed with staff.

Teachers report diminishing confidence about teaching class music since the retirement of Mrs Elgar. I would like to explore the possibility of employing a part-time specialist music instructor. This may also help us to deliver PPA more effectively.

PREPARING A REPORTING SCHEDULE

A well-organised governing body will include a timetable for monitoring and evaluation within its schedule of work. Some monitoring, such as Special Educational Needs, Safeguarding Children, Race Equality policy and incidents of racial harassment, is required by law or by local authorities. There will also be issues that are a priority for your school; you may have a particular concern about pupil behaviour or gifted and talented children and wish to receive reports on them. By agreeing this timetable at the start of the year you can ensure a manageable spread of work through the year and give plenty of notice for relevant people to produce it. It gives everyone the chance to see the overall reporting pattern, to ensure that it represents a reasonable call on the time of headteacher and others, that it relates to the issues that you have agreed are important for your school and that the governing body will know what to do with it when it arrives!

Some of the reporting will be direct to the full governing body; others will be better directed to a specific committee where there should be time for more detailed questioning and discussion.

Here is an example of the format for a monitoring and evaluation schedule:

Reporting on	Full gov. body	Committee (Specify)	Date
Incidents of racial harassment	✓		Report at next meeting. Annual analysis in June
Pupil achievement		Curriculum	
Safeguarding children annual review	✓		June
Quality of teaching and learning		Curriculum	Feb.
Budget monitoring		Resources	Oct./Feb./June
Evaluation of new management structure		Resources	June
Progress on School Development Priority 1 – Gifted & Talented		Curriculum	Feb./June
Progress on School Development Priority 2 – Remodelling Key Stage 1 Area		Resources	Feb.

HELPING TO FOCUS GOVERNING BODY DISCUSSION

It helps governors focus on the content of reports if heads put sentences in bold type at the ends of key paragraphs recommending what the governing body should do with the information.

- "The governing body is asked to note the reasons given above for the delay in implementing the .... policy and to accept the suggested revised timescale."
- "The governing body is asked to note the improvements achieved in this area and the lessons learned from this successful strategy."
- "The governing body is advised to set up a small working party to consider how the school might respond and to report back by .... [date]".
- "The governing body is advised to allocate some time next Autumn to discuss the issue."

Reporting/accounting to the governing body 33

GOVERNORS HAVE A RESPONSIBILITY FOR QUALITY REPORTING TOO

If governors expect headteachers to take care over the production of their reports they have an obligation to be conscientious in exercising their own more limited responsibilities for reporting to the governing body. The most obvious of these are reports arising from the work of governing body committees. It may well be that those committee meetings have drawn heavily on the information and advice provided by headteacher and staff, but if the committee has had any point at all, it will have been to do something useful with it – whether it be to make decisions or confirm that a policy is working well. So rehashing the head's advice is not good enough. Committees need to provide a written report of actions taken or key points from their own monitoring and evaluation – and this must not be left to the headteacher.

If an action has been taken by an individual governor with delegated powers an opportunity to report this should be clearly indicated in the agenda. These items will usually be for information only.

A list of possible items that may be requested by the governing body for inclusion in reports – from headteachers or others – is included in the Annex to this chapter (pages 35–6).

Reporting on pupil achievement

Most governing bodies have a committee dealing with the curriculum and this will often dedicate an autumn meeting to considering their headteacher's analysis of Key Stage assessments (including GCSEs, GNVQs and A levels) and to using RAISEonline data. Such meetings give ample time for good discussion. Often, the same analysis is presented to the next full governing body meeting and the headteacher is again expected to provide explanations. A committee which takes itself seriously will, instead, produce its own report for the full governing body, presenting the most important points that arose from the discussion of the head's analysis. This serves two purposes: it forces committee members to understand the analysis and to keep asking questions until they do, and it provides all governors with an incisive and usually more memorable summary to inform their view of how well the school is doing.

Some might object that doing it this way deprives governors who are not members of the curriculum committee of the opportunity to discuss the detailed analysis. The answer is to issue an open invitation to all governors to attend this particular committee meeting.

The governing body's share in reporting to stakeholders

It must sometimes feel that all the effort at providing information falls to the headteacher and staff. I hope that this chapter has demonstrated that governors need to be sensitive in the demands they make and use the information they receive to maximum effect. But there's another way in which the balance of effort can be redressed. The governing body's reporting to parents, pupils, staff and other stakeholders is something that should be separated from the headteacher's operational communication with these groups. Governors should take responsibility for consulting on issues, communicating key decisions and reporting the impact of their policies. Governing bodies may ask to include a "Governors' Corner" in regular school newsletters or make use of a school noticeboard aimed at pupils and staff. They may hold open meetings for parents when there are specific issues to discuss. They may find that attending parents' consultation events provides a good opportunity to talk and listen to parents. In these ways they will be helping promote the school as parent-friendly.

Enhancing the reporting role of staff governors

Staff should hear about the governing body decisions from the headteacher and staff governors. If governing bodies take communication with all the staff seriously they and the headteacher will find ways to support staff governors to do it. Some staff governors are reticent about reporting because they are not confident that they will be able to do it as clearly as their headteacher. Of course, that will be true if they never try. There is a quite commonly held view, too, that staff governors are not fully functioning governors, but it is in the interests of all governors that staff governors are both enabled and expected to be equal partners with every single other governor. As members of staff, these governors are managed by the headteacher; as members of the governing body they are part of a corporate body which manages the head.

A good headteacher will work with staff governors on a strategy for promoting an understanding of the governing body – what it does and how it operates – as well as reporting the decisions made at the meetings.

EFFECTIVE HEADTEACHERS	EFFECTIVE GOVERNING BODIES
Take reporting to the governing body seriously.	Take their heads' reports seriously.
Ensure that reports are produced in good time.	Ensure that committee reports are produced in good time.
Work with the governing body to plan what information it needs at different times through the year.	Work with their headteachers to plan what information they need at different times through the year.
Provide all the information that the governing body has requested according to the agreed timetable.	Take care that their requests are both reasonable in terms of workload and reasoned in that they are helpful to their role.
Highlight what they expect the governing body to do with different parts of the information they provide.	Work through their headteacher's reports methodically to ensure they make full use of the information.
Report to governing body (or committee) on matters delegated.	Ensure that committees and individual governors report back on delegated matters.
Prepare monitoring information as requested for the governing body.	Record monitoring information and discussion at committee level.
Do not report on matters that have already gone to committee.	Ensure committees report on issues already discussed with the headteacher.
Evaluate policies and initiatives against predicted outcomes.	Use evaluation reports as a learning exercise and to inform future action.
Restrict background information and explain predicted outcomes.	Use the background information received or ask for less to be produced in the future.
Offer space in the school's newsletter for a Governors' Corner and check for accuracy	Use school newsletters to report from the governing body to parents (and pupils).
Encourage governors to meet parents at Parent Consultation evenings etc.	Establish a rota to ensure a governor presence at every Parent Consultation evening in the year
Encourage staff governors to report governing body information to staff.	Encourage staff governors to report governing body information to staff.

ANNEX: REPORTING TO THE GOVERNING BODY – BY HEADTEACHER, COMMITTEES AND INDIVIDUAL GOVERNORS

The report items listed below are examples which represent the range of issues that a governing body may receive information on. It is up to the governing body and headteacher to decide which of these should be received, when and from whom.

Type of information	Example
Decisions or actions made using delegated powers	Admissions decisions (VA or Foundation Schools) Chair's urgent action Review of Health & Safety arrangements on premises Statistics on accidents and near misses Fund-raising Action taken by the headteacher using delegated powers (that are not covered elsewhere) Complaints Pupil exclusions Pupil exclusion appeals
Decision information	Options and recommendations on structure for staffing responsibilities Budget options and recommendations Analysis of pupil and parent views on school improvement priorities Identification of emerging priorities for school improvement Consideration of pros and cons of altering time of school day to ease transport arrangements Consideration of significant premises development project Requests for approval of school visits and journeys Local authority targets requiring action at school level Recommendations for pupil attainment targets* Plans for maintenance and replacement of major items, e.g. computers Information on local and national initiatives and policy developments that require urgent attention
Monitoring of specific decisions	Budget monitoring report Progress on School Development Plan – specific items depending on SDP timescales Progress on significant premises developments Policy monitoring information according to agreed arrangements Analysis of take-up of services provided for the community Review of Performance Management policy* and impact on quality of teaching & learning Staff development
Evaluation of specific decisions	Evaluation of the impact of each item in the School Development Plan Evaluation of significant premises development project Pupil attainment compared with targets previously agreed – with commentary if appropriate

School self-evaluation	Key issues (strengths and weaknesses) arising from analysis of pupil achievement Quality of teaching & learning Evidence of the impact the school is having on the outcomes that were introduced by Every Child Matters: • Stay safe • Be healthy • Enjoy and achieve • Make a positive contribution • Achieve future economic well-being Analysis of volume, coverage and impact of school visits Analysis of volume, coverage and impact of extra curricular activities Foundation Stage Profile results/KS2 results profile of new Year 7 entrants Report of any incidents of racial harassment* Outcomes of reviews of curricular areas Pupil attendance data* with trends and commentary if significant Pupil exclusion data analysed by type, gender and ethnic group Pupil & parent views of school performance Review of inclusion (including Race Equality and Disability Discrimination) and SEN policy* Analysis of complaints (different levels) and what the school has done to address them. "Notes of visit" from local authority advisers/officers or SIP Adequacy of resources to ensure curriculum access Community links including community use of premises and profile of hirings
Background information	Achievements of pupils and other members of school community Leavers' destinations* Staffing structure with changes in allocation of responsibility (if any) and deployment of senior management time. Year-on-year trends for admissions/applications and projected pupil numbers Staff changes, resignations, vacancies, appointments and numbers of applications Staff attendance data and trends – as an indication of health and well-being Information on local and national initiatives and policy developments which will impact on the life and work of the school in the future.

5. SCHOOL SELF-EVALUATION

How heads and governing bodies can help each other to clarify how well the school is doing

School self-evaluation lies at the core of school strategy. It must inform school development priorities; it is the background against which all other key decisions are made; and it is now very much the starting point for Ofsted inspection.

Ofsted can take some credit for the improved ability of schools to evaluate themselves in recent years. The evolving Ofsted frameworks have provided school leadership teams with clear criteria to make robust judgements, and the Self-Evaluation Form that Ofsted introduced enabled schools to record and update those judgements. As I pointed out in my book *School Self-Evaluation, Improvement and Inspection: A practical guide for school governors* (Adamson Publishing, 2012), self-evaluation is important for the school and is not something governors do just to satisfy Ofsted. But the clarity that Ofsted has provided in the descriptors contained in the evaluation framework make it much easier for heads and governors to make judgements.

Governing bodies should ensure that their school self-evaluation focuses particularly on:

- Pupil outcomes, including:

    how well do pupils achieve and enjoy their learning?

    pupils' wellbeing

    pupils' spiritual, moral, social and cultural development

- The effectiveness of provision, including the quality of teaching, use of assessment, curriculum, care, guidance and support

- The effectiveness of leadership & management, including:

    the contribution of leadership at all levels in the school to communicating ambition and driving improvement

    the governing body challenging and supporting the school so that weaknesses are tackled decisively and statutory responsibilities met

    promoting equal opportunity, tackling discrimination and safeguarding children

    engaging with parents and carers

    forming partnerships and promoting community cohesion

    deploying resources to achieve value for money

- The effectiveness of the Early Years Foundation Stage or Sixth Form as appropriate.

GOVERNING BODIES CANNOT LEAVE SCHOOL SELF-EVALUATION TO THE HEADTEACHER

School self-evaluation appears to be a complex process which is best left to the professionals, and indeed the collection and analysis of most data is very definitely an operational task for school leadership teams. Headteachers may feel that they and their colleagues should be left to get on with self-evaluation, involving outside professionals such as the School Improvement Partner, and that governors should be satisfied merely with the knowledge that it is being done. Governors may share the view that it is too complex for lay people to understand and that the best way to ensure that it is done effectively will be to keep out of their head's way.

However understandable these attitudes may be, they are unhelpful both to headteachers and governing bodies. Explaining to governors encourages heads to reflect on their judgements and clarify their thinking. Headteachers need their governing body to be well-informed about the school's strengths and weaknesses if it is to make good decisions. Governing bodies are ultimately accountable for the standards in their schools and the increasingly hands-off approach of local government means it is even more important they know their school well. Therefore, a governing body that wants to be helpful to the school leadership and make key strategic decisions on the basis of a deep and shared understanding will take an active role in school self-evaluation and not merely passively receive reports prepared by the leadership team.

As already noted, school self-evaluation covers a wide range of topics, so governing bodies are advised to work on this a bit at a time. Different committees can consider specific pieces at different times during the school year and report back to the full governing body.

Pupil attainment and progress, including those of pupils with learning difficulties and/or disabilities may be most appropriately considered by the curriculum committee in the autumn term after the analysis of Key Stage results and other assessments has been discussed. What would we want to say about this aspect of school and how would we wish to change our current self-evaluation statement to reflect our present position?

Personal development and well-being and **the quality of provision** (teaching and learning, the curriculum, and care, guidance and support) are also for the curriculum committee and may be scheduled for consideration in the spring and summer terms. Judgements on the quality of teaching and learning will emerge from classroom monitoring, which was described in chapter 4.

Leadership and management covers many issues that could be dealt with by the full governing body, but some could be shared between committees, e.g.:

- How effectively resources are deployed is a judgement for the resources committee but value for money depends on pupil outcomes which involves the curriculum committee.

- Judgements on equal opportunity and discrimination, the impact of community cohesion and effectiveness of partnerships to promote learning and well-being may fall under the remit of the curriculum committee.

Governor involvement in collecting and analysing the views of pupils and parents ...

The increasing realisation that school effectiveness requires more and deeper engagement with parents and the pupils themselves makes the governing body's role in consulting, discovering views and actively considering them all the more important. It is possibly the most direct indication of the governing body's effectiveness in fulfilling its accountability role. This is therefore an aspect of school self-evaluation which the governing body should be intimately involved with on a regular basis. Headteachers should encourage their governors to consider a variety of strategies to ascertain views. This may involve hearing directly from stakeholders, considering views collected by school staff and analysing unsolicited compliments or complaints. The governing body needs to agree what views are to be collected, from whom and by whom, how they will be collected and how they will be analysed. It should establish a schedule for doing this, both to ensure that this information is collected at the most convenient times and that the analysis of results can be fed into the appropriate governing body meeting.

The schedule should also include any process for analysing and reporting compliments, concerns and complaints. Of course, concerns and complaints have to be dealt with speedily when they occur, but identifying trends and drawing lessons is a longer-term task. An effective organisation welcomes complaints as a way of being alerted to what needs improving, and follows them up to find how quickly and efficiently they have been handled.

... and other stakeholders

Staff are stakeholders. Their careers and job satisfaction are affected by the policies and practices adopted by the governing body. Do governors know their views? Staff governors should be the conduit, but you cannot assume they always will be without some effort from the whole governing body. Headteachers can make the process easier by being open and relaxed about staff expressing their views and forestall any issues before they are revealed in any formal questionnaires.

In voluntary schools the **foundation** – usually a religious group – is a stakeholder. How much does the congregation know about what is happening in their school and how are their views fed in? Similarly to the situation with staff, the foundation governors should be the conduit of information, but the full governing body with the encouragement of the headteacher may need to make particular efforts to ensure that this happens.

The **local authority** has views. In the past LA concerns have sometimes stopped with the head and chair of governors. Then governors have been surprised when storms have blown in from an apparently cloudless sky. All governors should know about the local authority's view of their school, especially if it has identified problems. By sharing the contents of all relevant – and non-confidential – judgements by the LA, headteacher and chair can give fellow governors confidence that there are no lurking issues and the impetus to start tackling them if there are.

EFFECTIVE HEADTEACHERS	EFFECTIVE GOVERNING BODIES
Set aside sufficient time for effective school self-evaluation.	Help heads to schedule time for school self-evaluation – if necessary by allocating additional management time.
Help their governing body to schedule the review of different aspects of the school.	Work with headteachers to schedule the governing body's review of different aspects of the school.
Provide governors with analysis from school self-evaluation about the strengths and weaknesses of the school.	Invest time to understand the main conclusions from school self-evaluation.
Assist the governing body to consult stakeholders.	Consult stakeholders to inform judgements about how well the school is doing.
Help staff governors to consult their colleagues on appropriate issues	Give staff governors the space to feed back views of other staff as part of school self-evaluation.

6. WORK-LIFE BALANCE AND WELL-BEING

How governors can improve their headteachers' work-life balance, and how headteachers can help them

There are very few governors who will not be concerned about the pressures that headteachers face in leading and managing their schools. Most of them are aware of their governing body's duty of care as employer (in effect in all schools) to do what it can to avoid staff distress.

Summary of the duties of an employer

To take positive steps to ensure the safety of the employee

To follow current recognised good practice

To keep abreast of developing knowledge

To weigh up risks against the cost and inconvenience of precautionary measures

---

There is rightly a lot of concern about the number of headteachers who suffer stress-related illness and are forced into premature retirement, and about the difficulties of recruiting new headteachers because of the stress associated with the job. Governors have a legal responsibility "to have regard to the work-life balance of the headteacher". The 2009 Staffing Regulations define this as "the head teacher being able to achieve a satisfactory balance between the time spent discharging the professional duties of a head teacher and the time spent by the head teacher pursuing personal interests outside work". Headteachers have the responsibility "to have regard to the work-life balance of the rest of the staff". The danger is that in conscientiously meeting their own responsibility to the rest of the staff, headteachers will take more tasks on themselves.

Governor awareness and empathy on their own will make little difference, and governors are often at a loss to know how they can improve the situation. In fact, they need headteachers to advise them about the issues and to help explore strategies for ameliorating pressures and improving well-being. It is important to remember that every individual has a prime responsibility for their own work-life balance and well-being, and that it is only the individual who can really understand the combination of pressures that apply to them. It is often easier to rail against the impossibility of a situation than to take the time to analyse it thoroughly and work out how it might be improved. If you really want to help your headteacher you need to be quite firm in asking the appropriate questions; you need to provide the space for them to reflect on their situation; you need to listen both to the problem and the suggestions or clues about how the problem may be relieved. And you must be prepared to consider changing your own practices if that may help.

THE CHAIR'S ROLE

The greater the pressures, the more difficult it is to take corrective action, so early intervention, as in most things, is the best policy. In most schools the chair of governors meets regularly with the headteacher to mull over issues, act as a sounding board and plan for effective governing body working. This, in itself, can help to reduce stress and promote well-being and it can also provide early warning of dangerously increased stress. Chairs should know what emergency help is available and try to ensure that it is used.

UNDERSTANDING THE THINGS HEADTEACHERS AND GOVERNORS CANNOT CHANGE – BUT AVOIDING VICTIMHOOD

National initiatives and targets

Many elements of extra workload emanate from national government – a price to be paid for education being high on the government's agenda. Initiatives often come with tight deadlines and additional targets, and it is easy to feel yourself a victim, buffeted by change. However, there are strategies that headteachers and governors can adopt to take some control over these external pressures. In particular, having a strong sense of vision and values can help exploit useful initiatives and screen out the least helpful features of others. In addition, the Training and Development Agency (TDA) produced some good advice to help schools manage change, including the establishment of Change Teams with representatives of staff at all levels and governors.

Resources are finite

Tight budgets can appear to prevent the school from doing any of the things it really wants. There are, of course, relatively few opportunities to increase a school's income. This means that the deployment of resources is vital, but continuing your school's historic spending patterns may not be the best way to do this. So the answer to anyone – governor or head – who says, "We would love to do X but our budget makes it impossible," is to ask, "Let's take a long hard look at our budget and discuss how we might deploy resources differently." This gets governors and headteachers to discuss strategic priorities and how to achieve them.

FACTORS CONTRIBUTING TO STRESS – AND HOW TO ADDRESS THEM

The Health and Safety Executive has identified a wide range of factors that affect stress and well-being. These include the obvious ones such as overload and excessive hours, lack of control and lack of resources, and also less obvious ones that relate to training and support, sense of achievement, culture and relationships. It is possible for governing bodies and headteachers to do something positive to affect all of these. While they cannot sweep all the stresses away, they can create conditions where headteachers are more likely to agree with the statements below.

"I rarely feel overloaded and don't have to work excessively long hours"

Overload and working excessively long hours may seem like a fact of educational life. A survey of 68 headteachers found that they were working an average of 57.6 hours per week when the Health Education Authority recommends that for a healthy weekly balance work should take up 25-30 percent of the week (approximately 45 hours) and the Working Time Regulations require that 48 hours averaged over a 17-week period should not be exceeded. Working excessively long hours over a prolonged period rarely leads to the most effective working and increases the risk of burn-out. However, it is the professionalism and perfectionism of many staff in schools that contribute to long hours; after all, in education it is never possible to say the job is complete. So a recognition that headteachers and staff serve children best when they are fresh and rested, and that putting a realistic limit on evening and week-end work is not shirking, should act as an inducement to identify those tasks where "good enough" rather than perfection is a professionally sound judgement.

Governors can ask questions that suggest possible ways of improving the situation. In particular, can the headteacher delegate more? This may require the governing body to divert resources to fund additional management time and training, while in very small schools where headteachers have no one to delegate to, the answer may lie in sharing staff across a group of schools. There can be numerous reasons why these strategies may be deemed to be impractical or unaffordable, but the price is nothing compared to coping with long-term sickness – so where are the governing body's priorities?

"The governing body does not place excessive demands on my time and energy"

Governors will also recognise that they contribute to demands on their headteacher. You will do no one any favours if you over-react to the point of holding back on exercising your legitimate role, but there are some things you can consider that might help to reduce the strain:

- Can we reduce the number of meetings our headteacher has to attend by having fewer committees or fewer full governing body meetings?
- Could some or all of our meetings be earlier in the day?
- Can we ensure that no meeting lasts more than two hours?
- Have we agreed clear priorities with our headteacher?
- Are we asking our headteacher for the information we really need, and do we give plenty of notice?
- Are our meetings well-focused and constructive?

Conflicting priorities and tight deadlines are major stress factors for headteachers. A really strategic governing body will help to clarify priorities and, by planning ahead, will reduce the number of tight deadlines.

And as a governor him- or herself, the headteacher should play a full part in discussing these questions and seeking ways to achieve improvements.

"I feel I'm doing a good job"

None of the above will prevent the headteacher's job being a hugely demanding and onerous one. However, it will help if they feel they are achieving things they can be proud of, and that their efforts are really appreciated. It is important that governors consider what they can do to make the headteacher's work satisfying and even enjoyable. By responding to monitoring reports in the way described in chapter 3, they can help make it so.

Throughout, this book has aimed to show how governing bodies can operate to ensure that in working together with the headteacher they can really make a difference and thoroughly justify the effort that is undoubtedly involved in the role. If governors cannot only ensure that the demands the governing body makes on their headteacher are not excessive, but that those demands really do help the head to lead a more successful school, the work becomes more tolerable. As many readers will have experienced, fatigue often occurs when you are engaged in a task you regard as a pointless chore, whereas you can work energetically for hours on a much more demanding job that you believe is really important.

The headteacher's performance management is a perfect opportunity for the two or three governors involved to recognise the importance of his or her work over the past year. When governors, headteacher and SIPs take performance management as seriously as it deserves and engage in well-informed dialogue about the previous year and agree relevant and realistic targets for the next year, the whole process becomes an affirmation of the importance of both head and governing body. The most demoralising way to treat the process is to do it in a last-minute rush which undervalues not only performance management itself but the headteacher's role in leading the school. Governing bodies need to make sure that the governors it chooses to carry out the performance management role are fully committed, well trained and have the time to prepare properly for this key task.

"I feel competent and properly trained"

It is not selfish for headteachers to focus on their own training needs if this enables them to acquire the skills to lead more effectively. The governing body should ensure that there is sufficient provision in the budget for headteachers to receive training.

"I can find a sympathetic ear or helping hand"

The chair of governors has an important role to play as confidant(e) of the headteacher but there needs to be a wider range of support.

Headship can be a very lonely job and it probably feels more lonely as the pressures build. Many headteachers form mutual support groups through which a head can pick up the phone and discuss an issue or talk through a problem with a trusted colleague. The headteacher associations also offer advice services. Headteachers who are most in need of this support are often the least likely to use it, but the chair of governors might be the most appropriate person to encourage their head to get into and use such networks.

"We're encouraged to learn from mistakes"

As discussed in chapter 3, a "no-blame culture" is healthy in the relationship of head and governors and across the school.

"People treat me with dignity and respect"

Being treated with dignity and respect can make a huge difference to the way people perceive their workload. Chapter 2 suggested ways in which governing bodies can build constructive relationships with headteachers based on mutual respect. The critical friend role of the governing body also involves being an advocate for the school, and sometimes the governing body may need to express their respect publicly and model the respect to headteacher and staff that it expects pupils and parents to exhibit. It is also good to find a way of encouraging parents, pupils (and staff) to be more generous with "thank yous" when appropriate. Some organisations display letters of appreciation in their reception area.

A very few over-demanding parents can be the cause of major stress. The chair may help alleviate this: perhaps by encouraging the head to forestall trouble by being more open when appropriate, or by communicating firm messages to the parent if necessary. The "critical friend" skill is in deciding which of these options is appropriate!

"GETTING A LIFE"

So far this chapter has focussed on the work side of the work-life equation. Important elements on the "life" side include health, family and friends, and leisure. The Health Education Authority recommends spending 20-25 percent of your week (approximately 39 hours) on leisure activities. The survey of 68 headteachers found they were managing an average of 5.2 hours leisure per week. There is only a little that governors can do about this, but they can, for example, avoid making late night telephone calls to the head, and can take an interest in them as an individual – without prying!

As confidant(e), the chair of governors might in certain circumstances encourage the head to take up another leisure pursuit which takes him or her out of the house and away from the desk for one evening per week. Work will always flow into a vacuum and a specific leisure commitment may be the only thing that forces it out.

The performance management process is a key opportunity for the appropriate governors to discuss work-life balance issues with their headteacher and, if necessary, to agree strategies designed to make a real difference.

When governors appoint their next headteacher they would be well-advised to find out what candidates do to "switch off". The national guidance on safer recruiting advises selection panels to ask candidates about their coping strategies.

First aid

Prevention is better than cure but if, despite these efforts, governors feel that their headteacher is likely to be in distress, headteachers and chairs of governors should know where to seek emergency support. The local authority Human Resource staff are likely to be the first port of call. They will provide information on how to access Occupational Health and its counselling service if that is appropriate. Headteachers should be advised to refer themselves – in the same way that they would advise any member of staff in that position to refer themselves – but if necessary the chair of governors can make the referral.

WHAT ABOUT GOVERNOR WORK-LIFE BALANCE AND WELL-BEING?

This chapter has focused deliberately on the headteacher's work-life balance and the way that governors and headteachers should work together to address it. Governors work hard too, but as they are volunteers their governor work sits in the "life" part of the balance. Nevertheless, for some governors, especially chairs, the work can be very complex and time-consuming. Other governors have a responsibility to share some of that load. Volunteering in general is good for well-being but governing will only have that beneficial effect if governors feel that their volunteering is making a difference. That is why heads and governors must plan together to

---

Volunteering is good for well-being

Research has revealed that people who volunteer appear to be happier than those who don't. But the question then arises: do they volunteer because they are happy people or does volunteering make them happier?

The fall of the Berlin Wall gave researchers a chance to unpick these factors. Many of the opportunities for volunteering in the former East Germany disappeared in the two following years. Researchers were able to measure how the happiness of people who had lost their volunteering role changed compared with others who had not volunteered in the first place. They found that there was a significantly greater decline in the happiness of the volunteering population.

Evan Davies, who reported this research for the BBC, concluded: "Volunteering is so good for well-being that it ought to be made compulsory!"

address the key strategic issues that will make the biggest difference to the school as described in chapter 1, and establish healthy relationships, as described in chapter 2.

Promoting wellbeing

Headteachers and governing bodies should consider making staff wellbeing a priority, in the long-term interest of all the pupils. A happy, healthy and well-motivated staff who are encouraged to identify the ways they could work more effectively will provide a better education for pupils and increase parent satisfaction. A research study into the links between staff wellbeing and school performance suggested that "there is a two-way relationship between teacher wellbeing and pupil performance. Just as increases in teacher wellbeing can lead to improvements in the performance of pupils, so increases in pupil performance may lead to increased wellbeing in teachers. *(Staff Wellbeing is Key to School Success*, R. Briner and C. Dewberry, Birkbeck College, 2007; www.worklifesupport.com).

Governor well-being should spring from an awareness of a volunteering job well done.

Effective headteachers	Effective governing bodies
Take responsibility for their own work-life balance.	Have regard to the head's work-life balance.
Are prepared to recommend and problem-solve ways to improve their work-life balance	Insist the head reflects on and reports on work-life balance issues.
Work with the governing body to plan work and avoid bunching.	Work with head to plan schedule of work to avoid bunching.
Use their management time effectively.	Ensure they have budgeted for sufficient management time.
Help the governing body to review its meetings, etc.	Review governing body meetings and committees to see if they could be fewer or shorter or start earlier.
Play their part in helping the governing body to work more effectively	Work effectively to make their head's time with governors more rewarding.
Provide the information that enables governors to offer praise and encouragement.	Use all opportunities to offer praise and encouragement.
Model respect for colleagues.	Demonstrate respect for head and staff.
Take their performance management seriously.	Take performance management of the headteacher seriously.
Find effective ways to "switch off" and carve out personal time to do it!	Take an interest in their head as a person – without prying.
Don't feel guilty about early nights!	Avoid late night phone calls and don't expect late night responses to emails.
Use support networks before problems become critical.	Encourage the headteacher to use networks.
Use the chair of governors as a sounding board.	The chair is prepared to listen and respond to soundings.
Alert the chair to their distress if they can, and accept help.	Look out for signs of distress and know where to seek help.

7. WORKING WITH NEW RELATIONSHIPS

How headteachers and governing bodies can exploit the opportunities and avoid the pitfalls

Headteachers and governing bodies are operating in a different and dynamic environment. Children's Services replaced local authority Education Departments to reflect the need arising from the previous government's Every Child Matters agenda for seamless provision of services for children, young people and families. For some time now governments have increasingly defined the role of local authorities as the commissioning (rather than the provision) of educational services, the championing of children, young people and families, and intervention in schools only to avoid failure. National government keeps promising to interfere less and to leave schools more freedom to take decisions.

This does not leave schools in splendid isolation. They are being encouraged to club together to take greater advantage of their new freedoms, to share expertise, spread good practice and raise pupil attainment. Headteachers and school staff are expected to engage in multi-agency working for the early identification and intervention in children's educational and non-educational needs.

These trends will have major implications for leadership and governance. Tempting as it may be, they cannot be ignored. All the same, schools are not obliged to adopt slavishly everything that it is now possible to do, but should exercise choice. It is important that headteachers and all governors develop a shared understanding of the changing environment and find time to explore what it means for their school. This chapter will highlight ways in which the changes may affect how the headteacher and governing body currently work and point up the opportunities for strengthening the partnership.

KEEPING UP WITH INFORMATION

The blizzard of paper from national government is supposed to abate as a result of web-based communication. Many local authorities are also trying to achieve reductions. There are potential advantages in this but there is a danger that, because they have to seek information rather than receive it, governors – and sometimes busy heads – will miss some vital piece. It is essential, therefore, that the governing body establishes a robust system of accessing and assessing information. It may be an opportunity for the chair to share out some of the initial reading – with the vice-chair or other interested individual, or with all governors on an agreed rotation.

A DIFFERENT RELATIONSHIP WITH THE LOCAL AUTHORITY

Headteachers and governing bodies need to consider the practical implications of the changing relationship with their local authority. These will include:

- the local authority as a commissioner rather than provider of services
- the local authority as a "champion for children".

Local authorities ceasing to be providers

The government expects local authorities to be commissioners rather than providers of services – with schools now often having to commission people themselves to carry out that part of the school adviser role that deals with school improvement. Schools will still require other support and services but it is expected that a diminishing amount of that support will come directly from local authorities. Many governing bodies and their headteachers are already developing the skills to "shop around" for these services, and all will need to become more sophisticated as the trend develops further.

This involves having a clear understanding of what support the headteacher and staff and the governing body need, knowing where to find a range of providers of that support, knowing how to express your needs clearly and compare value for money offered by each provider, and doing all this quickly and efficiently so that it does not divert too much time and energy from the business of school improvement or discourage schools from seeking the help they need. Most of this is about implementation and is therefore a task for school staff under the direction of the head. The strategic role of governors is to ensure there are good systems for clarifying the needs, appropriate choices of provider, and effective methods of judging value for money so that headteachers can take decisions swiftly. Governing bodies will also wish to ensure there are clear monitoring processes so that lessons can be learned and fed back into future school commissioning processes.

This may be fairly straightforward for a large school with numerous staff but will be more difficult for the small village school. Here there are clear advantages in clubbing together in some way to share the commissioning and assessing of providers, and the strategic work of governing bodies in supporting and in some cases insisting on inter-school collaboration becomes vital.

The environment for support services is not static and will develop at different speeds in different parts of the country. Some local authorities may move fast to dismantle their own support services following the spirit of new legislation and/or responding to the expressed wishes and actions of schools in their area. In other local authorities the pace of this change may – for better or worse – proceed in a more stately fashion. But governing bodies will need to ensure that their antennae are well attuned to pick up the trends so that they are in a position to respond.

The local authority as a "champion for children"

Most local authorities publish a plan that sets targets for education and describe the actions required to achieve them. In their role as "champions for children", local authorities are expected to work with schools to deliver as much of their strategy as is appropriate, and to contribute to effective inter-agency working. While there are few issues over which LAs can direct schools, governing bodies and heads of maintained schools are expected to cooperate with the LA and others for the benefit of children in the area.

The implications for governing bodies is that they need to know the overall targets in their local plan, understand how outside agencies expect to contribute and what the school thinks it can do. Multi-agency working is mostly about operational matters, but governors have an advocacy role in bringing school and agencies together if they believe agencies could do more to help schools achieve their targets. They also need to be aware of the resource implications, identify other barriers and consider strategies for overcoming them.

Autonomy, inter-dependence and cooperation

While aiming to dismantle schools' dependence on their local authority, the government's aim is not to cut schools off from each other but to encourage collaborative working between them. This is even, or maybe even especially, the case with academies, which are expected to work with struggling schools, while the government also promotes the development of academy chains, where the schools can benefit both from a single, central trust and also from the experiences of each other.

Collaborative arrangements can take many forms. They can be as simple as heads and governors from a number of schools coming together to discuss common issues, or they may involve sharing headteachers, federating two or more schools under a single governing body, setting up trusts to govern two or more schools, or forming Education Improvement Partnerships.

There is now a plethora of options, some of which may seem exciting or inviting and others bemusing or plain off-putting. Remember, there is no obligation to use them at all. It is rather like the range of programmes offered in a washing machine: most of us only use a programme for the white wash and another for coloured, but when we need to do something special like washing the curtains we can look up the manual and find the appropriate setting. But given the host of strategic challenges described in the Annex to chapter 1, it would be unwise to rule any of the options out on the grounds that you want to carry on as you are.

Moreover, you may not think there is any need for collaboration at the moment and feel that it is a complication that you can do without. However, if you wait until there is an urgent need to work with other schools you may find it impossible in a short time to build the trust and understanding that you require to get started. And in fact there are already important issues that schools need to address where talking with other governing bodies is important. While your school reaps the benefits of a stronger network, governing bodies will also be laying firm foundations upon which later collaboration might be built.

The firm ground on which headteachers and governors have become used to operating is shifting. Holes are opening up which may swallow the unwary, but there are fresh opportunities for the alert and strategic. As they are at the heart of the educational system headteachers may be best placed to inform their governors about the changing scene, but only if governors ensure the head has time for reflection and provide encouragement by showing an interest in these matters. However, the headteacher may be the cautious, conservative one in the partnership, reluctant to engage with change. In that case the governing body may need to challenge and push for a strategic response; and *vice versa* if the governing body is the reluctant one. Equally, either partner can be rash, wanting to rush headlong into new opportunities without considering the implications, in which case the other partner needs to act as a restraint. Whatever scenario applies, the correct response must be clear information, open discussion and reference back to the school's vision and values.

EFFECTIVE HEADTEACHERS	EFFECTIVE GOVERNING BODIES
Review their school's systems for dealing with web-based communication.	Review their governing body's systems for dealing with web-based and other electronic communication.
Keep their governing body informed appropriately about their analysis of pupil attainment and other data.	Keep developing their governing body's understanding of how the school analyses data and the conclusions it draws.
Find appropriate opportunities to involve governors in their meetings with the School Improvement Partner.	Grasp opportunities to involve themselves in the meetings with the School Improvement Partner.
Help their governing body to identify and judge the relative merits of different service providers.	Seek out the providers of support services who offer the school best value.
Use existing networks and, if appropriate, develop new ones to share the task of negotiating with new providers.	Use existing networks and, if appropriate, develop new ones to share the task of negotiating with new providers.
Are alert to changing relationships and keep the governing body informed.	Are alert to changing relationships.
Are alert to opportunities and expectations of multi-agency working required by the Every Child Matters agenda.	Consider how any barriers to effective multi-agency working can be overcome.
Exploit and further develop cross-school collaboration.	Invest time in developing good working relationships with other governing bodies to support cross-school collaboration.

8. DESERVE WHAT YOU GET

Headteachers, deserve your governors; governors, deserve your headteacher

It is sometimes said that headteachers get the governors they deserve, and *vice versa*. This book suggests that we should all set out to deserve the best of each other. Governors expect their headteacher to show leadership qualities, take the initiative, provide high-quality professional advice and run an effective school. Headteachers expect their governing body to take an interest in what they are trying to achieve, to share their understanding of the school's direction and allow them freedom and flexibility to get there. It is conceivable that these ideals might be realised without trying, but they usually need to be worked for. As we have seen, mutuality and reciprocity are the key.

Headteachers, develop your governing body

Joan Sallis has long asserted that developing their governing body is the last, great challenge for a headteacher who has achieved everything else. I say, don't leave it as the last challenge. Make it an early challenge because heads who achieve this will find it helps them to achieve all their other challenges. It is a shared challenge because governors who understand their role will want to develop themselves. However, governors sometimes think that they can fulfil huge obligations with little or no training. Headteachers who just shrug their shoulders and go along with this are making rods for their own backs. The onus for briefing will fall even more on them, and they will fail to harness the power that a governing body firing on all cylinders can generate. On the other hand, heads who attend governor training – more often now in-house or partnership sessions – will lead by example, will hear and be able to build on the key messages that governors learn. It is a good investment of their time if the training is of good quality; it may be even more important that heads attend if the training messages need to be clarified or corrected.

But governors must want to learn and must be prepared to invest time in identifying and seeking to meet their training needs. As explained in the early chapters, governors have a responsibility to everyone, including their headteachers, to ensure that they are properly trained and equipped. Where the governing body has nominated a training link or development governor this person should be capable of promoting this vital activity. If your governing body does not have a nominated governor the vice-chair may be the best person to take it on. The one person it should not fall to is the chair, who will already have too many other tasks. Moreover, the government is considering making training obligatory for clerks and chairs of governors.

Governors, develop your headteacher

It may seem obvious that the heads of learning organisations should not need to be reminded to undertake formal learning for themselves, but this is not always the case. Headteachers sometimes put the needs of their more junior colleagues first, or feel that they are too busy with day-to-day management, or that the budget cannot bear more days away from school, or that their work-life balance precludes any more evening events. All of these reasons may be perfectly valid. However, in their role as critical friend, the governing body can ensure that the school's training plan balances all factors. Even where there are none of these constraints, headteachers may need to be encouraged to put working with their governing body on the list of priority areas. Developing an understanding of governing bodies among staff who may be heads in future is also important. Clearly, if governors show that they take their own training and development seriously, they will be in a strong position to suggest that their headteacher does the same!

SUMMING IT UP

Readers who have come this far will have found some advice that has particular resonance with their school, together with some that they will regard as hopelessly idealistic or not applicable. The tool below aims to help you summarise the book's key messages and discuss with fellow governors the actions you might prioritise to make the partnership work more effectively.

Suggested actions	Done well (or well enough)	Not important	Action needed	Actions agreed
Agree schedule of key strategic tasks with your headteacher. (Chapter 1)				
Clarify delegation to your headteacher to ensure that the governing body can focus on the key strategic tasks. (Chapter 1)				
Review the ground rules for working in partnership to ensure that it is based on firm foundations. (Chapter 2)				
Promote a "no blame" culture across the school. (Chapter 3)				
Clarify (and schedule) the reports that the governing body wishes to receive from the head (and other school staff). (Chapter 4)				
Review how the governing body handles reports and agree improvements. (Chapter 4)				
Agree actions that the governing body will take to report governing body decisions to stakeholders. (Chapter 4)				
Consider ways the governing body can help your head with school self-evaluation. (Chapter 5)				
Discuss with your headteacher ways to improve their work-life balance. (Chapter 6)				
Identify actions to make best use of the School Improvement Partner. (Chapter 7)				
Consider how collaboration with other schools and agencies can help you and your head achieve your aims and agree action. (Chapter 7)				
Identify training needs to help make partnership more effective. (Chapter 8)				

9. TROUBLESHOOTING

What to do when the partnership breaks down

A successful partnership is not always easily achieved and, like a marriage, the relationship between a governing body and a headteacher may enter stormy seas and sail dangerously close to rocky shores. In these circumstances it is particularly important to think about the children and the possible effect on their education; this should help to put any transgressions into perspective and focus everybody on resolving differences and steering back into calmer waters.

The table below lists some of the things that can go wrong and what headteachers and governors might consider in response. Quiet reflection and discussion either between the chair of governors and the headteacher or within the full governing body will usually help to identify where the problem lies and point to an effective resolution.

If the problems persist you may need to consider counselling. If so, consult your Governor Services department for assistance.

Symptom	Issue	Consider
Governors can't find anything good to say about their headteacher	"Critical friend" balance of support and challenge not working	How did *you* let it get to this? You have a responsibility to help turn it round Everyone responds to praise and encouragement The benefits of a "no blame" culture (page 24) How to avoid demoralising your headteacher
	Headteacher capability (rare)	How did *you* let it get to this? You have a responsibility to help turn it round Ways to support and help headteacher to succeed
Headteacher can't find anything good to say about their governors.	Responding to over-challenging governors	How did *you* let it get to this? You have a responsibility to help turn it round Has lack of openness and defensiveness contributed to governor frustration? Sometimes clumsiness may make a question or statement feel more challenging than intended (page 26) Explaining to governors how their over-challenging behaviour makes you feel
	Ineffective governing body	Importance of encouraging and praising behaviours that will improve governor work Encouraging governor training How to develop governor skills internally

Troubleshooting

Symptom	Issue	Consider
The governing body gets bogged down in inappropriate detail so that it is unable to provide effective direction	Agenda unfocused	Prioritising strategic issues Providing information/reports that structure strategic discussions
	Renegade governor(s) with own agenda	Applying peer group pressure to insist on return to strategic priorities (pages 5–6) Insisting on training to explain why the behaviour is inappropriate
Governors expect the headteacher to do all the work – "We're only volunteers." Headteacher expects governing body to "rubber stamp". Headteacher doesn't believe governors have commitment or capacity to help the school – "They're only volunteers/amateurs."	Lack of commitment to partnership	Remembering that effective governing bodies help schools to achieve their aims (see Introduction) The power of high expectations Importance of mutual respect (page 20) Training for governors and headteacher Reviewing roles and responsibilities (chapter 1) Reviewing quality of information for governors Sensible division of work – shared across the whole governing body (page 21)
Headteacher and/or governors act as though there is too much to do to allow time for the "niceties" of partnership	Lack of commitment to partnership	See above
	Genuine overload	Prioritising key strategic tasks (page 12) Sharing the work (page 21) Lack of partnership working can impede progress
Headteacher has feeling of being bombarded by critical friend questioning, comments and suggestions on a wide variety of issues, in and out of meetings.	Each individual intervention may seem appropriate, but the accumulation of them will eat into headteacher time and nerves and is bound to impede their ability to lead	Treating some governor behaviour as clumsiness Prioritising key strategic tasks Direct energy of enthusiastic newcomers to the priorities Reviewing headteacher's work-life balance and encouraging head to express how it feels (pages 40–44) Maintaining the critical friend role but, if necessary, making it better focused (pages 15–16)
	Renegade governor may be causing trouble	Reminding governors and heads that no individual governor has any power unless delegated Focusing governors on the agenda and controlling AOB Using peer-group pressure to discourage behaviour that impedes or demoralises the headteacher
	May be a problem of how the head handles quite reasonable requests from governors	Reflecting on possible defensiveness in responding to requests (page 16) Reflecting on the benefits of governors who carry out an appropriate critical friend role (pages 15–16) Putting some governor behaviour down to clumsiness (page 26) Reviewing time management and delegation skills so that response does not always fall on the headteacher Expressing feelings to allow governors to reflect on the effect of their behaviour Using graciousness to model desired behaviour

Symptom	Issue	Consider
Things promised repeatedly not done by headteacher or chair or other governor	Overload	What lessons can be learned? Are expectations too high? Was the promise freely made or was it an unreasonable demand? Is assertiveness undeveloped so people make promises they cannot fulfil? Is the headteacher delegating effectively? Are governors sharing the work?
	Lack of commitment to teamwork	Reminding colleagues about how it feels when promises are repeatedly not fulfilled
Headteacher fails to implement a governing body decision.	Quality of the decision-making process	Was there sufficient discussion so that objections were properly considered? Should the issue be re-considered? Was there sufficient time for implementation?
Governors undermine or ignore earlier decisions	Corporate responsibility	Reminding colleagues that corporate responsibility applies to all governors (page 21) Reminding governors that re-hashing old arguments slows progress
Headteacher resents governing body refusal to accept a recommendation	Headteacher is the governing body's main professional adviser	Reviewing implications of mutual respect (page 20) Were governors involved at an early stage in thinking about the issue? (page 26) Were the recommendations clearly explained with other options considered? Were there good reasons to reject the recommendation?
Governing body fails to discuss a recommendation and merely rubber stamps	A governing body that approves without question will not be able to support the head and justify the decision if questioned.	Did the recommendation have sufficient accessible data to stimulate good-quality discussion? Is there an expectation that governing body will discuss serious issues? Was time allowed in the agenda?
Staff refuse to accept decision of an exclusion appeal panel to reinstate pupil	Staff understanding of role of governing body in hearing appeals	Explaining to staff that appeal panel is obliged to hear all evidence and make its judgement "without fear or favour" (pages 24–5)
	Staff lack understanding of governing body's legitimate role	Role of headteacher, other staff governors and all other governors in communicating the governing body role (pages 33–4)
	Staff lack trust in the governing body's judgement	How did *you* let it get to this? Has there been a history of poor decisions? Has the governing body made concerted efforts to explain its decisions? (page 34) Inviting staff to attend in-house governor training
Headteacher resents a governor panel's decision to uphold a complaint	Headteacher fallibility	We all make mistakes (page 24) Everyone in authority can be over-ruled on appeal (pages 24–5)
	Headteacher's understanding of role of governing body in hearing complaints	Recognising that complaints panel is obliged to hear all evidence and make its judgement "without fear or favour" (pages 24–5)

Symptom	Issue	Consider
Governors take up parental complaints or staff grievances	Misunderstanding of governor role	Appreciating that the governors are well-intentioned Reminding colleagues that parent and staff governors are not delegates Reminding governors of procedures for parents and staff to raise concerns (pages 21–2) Preventing AOB in agendas being used to raise complaints Identifying general issues which may be legitimate areas for governing body discussion
	Communication with parents and staff	Reminding all of complaints/grievance procedure and that the governing body panel is the *last* resort (pages 21–2)
Key information appears to have been withheld from governors	Communication of headteacher to governors	Was it a mistake/oversight? In which case forgive and learn from it Was there a good reason? Explain and learn from it
	Communication of chair of governors to other governors	Letters/reports sent to the chair are, in most cases, intended for sharing with governors Was it a mistake/oversight? In which case forgive and learn from it Was there a good reason? Explain and learn from it
	Relationship of School Improvement Partner to head and governing body	Role of SIP to support and challenge both headteacher and governing body Publicising dates of SIP visits planned a year ahead Ensuring that SIP reports are circulated and discussed at full governing body meetings
	Lack of trust	Have (some) governors given cause to doubt confidentiality in the past? What is the governing body doing about it? (page 21) Have (some) governors over-reacted to bad news in the past? (page 26) Value of a "no blame" culture Reminding colleagues of the power of high expectations and harnessing peer group pressure to rebuild trust
Confidential information leaks out	Possibly a genuine mistake	Reminding everyone of corporate responsibility Expressing disappointment rather than anger
	Sometimes a deliberate act (rare)	Reminding everyone of the damage to trust that such breaches cause. Using peer group pressure to express censure
Governors feel that important decisions are taken outside governor meetings	Clarity of delegation	Revisiting a delegation decision planner and/or terms of reference (page 14)
	Existence of "A teams" and "B teams"	How did *you* let it get to this? Organisation of governing body procedures is a matter for the full governing body Sharing out the work so all governors are equal
	"Cosy" relationship between headteacher and chair	Importance of chair as a sounding board for the headteacher (page 22) Head and chair discussing how issues can be presented to governors so as to encourage debate (pages 22–3)

INDEX

academies 48
accountability 10, 14–15
accounts 16
admissions 35
Advanced Skills Teacher 31
aims 11–12
appeals 22, 24–6

behaviour 26
blame 24, 43, 55
budget 13, 35, 41, 43, 51
Building Schools for the Future 19

Cambridge Review 18
chair of governors 8, 14, 21, 22, 23, 29, 37, 41, 43, 44, 45, 46, 52–5
challenges 17–19
Children Act 2004 17
Children and Young People's Plan 48
Children's Trusts 18
clerks 22, 23
collaboration 9, 48–9, 51
committees 32, 33, 38, 42
community 11, 12, 20
community cohesion 18
complaints 21, 22, 24–6, 35, 39, 55
confidentiality 21, 55
corporate responsibility 24, 54
critical friend 10, 15–16, 25, 43, 51, 52, 53
curriculum 18, 38

delegated powers 29, 33, 35

Education Reform Act 1988 5
evaluation 6, 26, 29, 30, 32, 33
Every Child Matters 9, 36, 46
exclusions 24–5, 35, 54
extended services 17, 18-19, 35
external advisers 47

fallibility 24–7
federations 19
foundation 39
Framework for Inspecting Schools 6

Governing the School of the Future 15
governors' services 52
grievances 21, 55

headteacher's report to governors 15, 28–9, 31, 35–6
Health and Safety 13, 36, 41
hero heads 7
Hume, David 20

inclusion 11
inspection 12, 37

leadership 6, 24–7, 37, 38, 46
leisure 44
link governor 50
local authority 17, 39, 46–8
local management of schools 5

management 6, 37, 38
monitoring 26, 29–30, 42
multi-agency working 48
mutual support 20

National College for Leadership in Schools and Children's Services 9, 19
National Governors' Association 6
National Remodelling Team 41
natural justice 24–5
newsletters 34
noticeboard 34

Occupational Health 44
Ofsted 5, 6, 7, 8, 12, 20, 37
operational issues 13, 14

parent governors 13
parents 12, 14, 20, 22, 25, 33, 35, 37, 38, 55
performance management 31, 43, 44, 47
policies 12–13, 33
Primary Capital Programme 19
pupil attainment/achievement 30, 32, 33, 35, 36, 38, 46
pupil attendance 11, 17, 36
pupils 33, 35, 37, 38–9

race equality 32
racial harassment 36
RAISEonline 33
recruitment and retention 19
reporting schedule 32
resources 17
respect 20, 43
Rose, Sir Jim 18

safeguarding 14, 17, 32, 37
Sallis, Joan 9, 18, 50
school development plan 12, 29, 30, 35, 47
school improvement plan *see* school development plan
school visits 35, 36
self-evaluation 30, 36, 37–9
single conversation, the 46–7
special educational needs 32, 36
staff 12, 20, 22, 33, 39, 55
staff governors 12, 20, 34, 39
staffing structure 36
stakeholders 11, 33, 37, 38, 39
standards 38
strategic decision-making 10–14, 16
sustainability 17

teaching and learning 31, 36
teaching assistants 31
training 43, 50, 51, 53
trust 21
trusts 48
21st Century Schools 9, 14

values 41, 49
vice-chair 50
views of parents and pupils 38–9
vision 11–12, 20, 41, 49
volunteering 17, 44

wellbeing 17, 37, 40–45
workforce remodelling 18–19
work-life balance 23, 40–45, 51, 53

BIBLIOGRAPHY

Adamson, Stephen, *Accountability: a practical guide for school governors*, Adamson Publishing, 2010 (2nd edn)

DfES, *Governing the School of the Future*, DfES, 2005

Managing the Work of the Governing Body, GLM (Governance, Leadership and Management), 2011 (4th edn), Adamson Publishing

Marriott, David, *Being Strategic: a practical guide for school governors*, Adamson Publishing, 2011 (3rd edn)

Martin, Jane & Ann Holt, *Joined-up Governance: making sense of the role of the school governor*, Adamson Publishing, 2010 (3rd edn)

Pounce, Martin, *School Self Evaluation, Improvement and Inspection: a guide for school governors*, Adamson Publishing, 2012

Sallis, Joan, *Heads in Partnership: working with your governors for a successful school*, Pearson, 2001